UNPLUGGED

Luddites' *Guide* TO

CYBERSECURITY

WHAT TO TEACH YOUR
Kids & Grandparents
BEFORE THEY ACCESS THE INTERNET

Raj Goel, CISSP
raj@brainlink.com | 917-685-7731
www.brainlink.com | www.rajgoel.com
www.linkedin.com/in/rajgoel

revision 1.1

"If you want a picture of the future, imagine a Roomba leaking pix of your home, forever" was originally published by Cory Doctorow at *http://boingboing. net/2015/05/25/if-you-want-a-picture-of-a-fut.html*

Reprinted with the permission of Cory Doctorow

"Beware The Little Sisters" was originally published by De Volkskrant at *http://www. volkskrant.nl/vk/nl/2844/ Archief/archief/article/detail/3394833/2013/ 02/16/Vrees-de-Little-Sisters.dhtml*

Reprinted with the permission of De Volkskrant's copyright team 3/11/2013.

"Watch and See" was originally published in ISC2's InfoSecurity Professional Magazine July/August 2014 Issue. Reprinted with permission.

"Googling Security and Privacy" was originally published in ISC2's InfoSecurity Professional Magazine, Issue #6. Reprinted with permission.

"Beyond Security Awareness" was originally published in ISC2's InfoSecurity Professional Magazine, Issue #19. Reprinted with permission.

"Welcome To The World Of Dating Sites" was originally published in ISC2's InfoSecurity Professional Magazine Jan/Feb 2015 Issue. Reprinted with permission.

TABLE OF *Contents*

Protect Your Home & Family 13

Right To Privacy In The 21St Century 35

The Banes Of Technology

Please send your feedback, comments and ideas to me at raj@brainlink.com

ABOUT
Raj Goel

BIOGRAPHY

Author, entrepreneur, IT expert and public speaker, Raj Goel is globally known as the go-to man in cyber security and privacy law. He is committed to educating individuals and organizations about online safety and how to protect their most important assets – people and data. His expert advice helps individuals, companies and conglomerates navigate their way through the world's ever-changing technology and increasingly complex IT compliance laws. He often appears in the media and at conferences world-wide to educate the public on cyber-security and digital privacy, a subject he is passionate about.

Security, Civil Liberties and Peace of Mind

When you need the right approach to complying with HIPAA/HITECH, PCI-DSS or simply protecting your assets, Raj Goel, as any of his loyal clients will tell you, is the man to call upon. Raj's credentials are impeccable. A 25-year veteran of the IT industry and an expert in online security, Raj has personally consulted with organizations ranging from Fortune 100 corporations to small family companies to governments world wide.

Raj is fueled by his passion for enhancing civil rights in cyberspace and his love of helping people keep themselves, their families and their companies safe online. He is available as a consultant and a public speaker and often sought after by major media outlets, companies and government agencies.

Rajesh Goel, CISSP
raj@brainlink.com
www.brainlink.com
www.linkedin.com/in/rajgoel
Twitter: @Rajgoel_NY

Please send your feedback, comments and ideas to me at raj@brainlink.com

RAJ GOEL

Acknowledgements

*I am grateful to a large number of people who
helped me in creating this book.*

First & foremost, my wife Sharon for supporting me in
yet another crazy endeavor.

Secondly, to my beautiful girls, who left Papa alone when he needed to
write. I'm sorry if I was a grumpy bear a few times.

My excellent team at Brainlink – THANK YOU, THANK YOU, THANK
YOU! Sharon, Shival, Jyoti, Crawls, Abhi, Lina, Emalee, Jason – you guys
gave me the freedom & support I needed to create this.

Dr. Gerry Goldhaber – THANK YOU for the excellent title!

A SPECIAL thank you to SARAH – you know this book would have been
impossible without you. Thank you for helping me build the content
hopper, thank you for managing the Brainlink marketing program and
keeping a thousand dragons at bay. You are a gem!

As always, I am indebted to my friends at Gotham and
proud to be a member of the Friars Club.

Thank you Cory Doctorow @doctorow, Dan Gillmor @dangillmor, Brian
Krebs @briankrebs, Chris soghoian @csoghoian for fighting the good
fight, the excellent reporting and memorable tweets. I remain your fan…

Please send your feedback, comments and ideas to me at raj@brainlink.com

MESSAGE TO THE
Reader

> *Freedom of speech is a principal pillar of a free government;*
> *when this support is taken away, the constitution of a free society is*
> *dissolved, and tyranny is erected on its ruins.*
>
> BENJAMIN FRANKLIN (NOV 17, 1773)

Inside the heart of every bureaucrat, politician and policeman lurks a petty tyrant. New laws beget new crimes and the cycle continues until we have a social movement that resets society. What's being done to our children and teenagers, with the criminalization of sexting, social media monitoring, school surveillance, and etc., in the name of "anti-terrorism" and "homeland safety" is un-American and unacceptable.

The rights that you and I enjoy – freedom of speech, freedom of religion, clean air, clean water, safe food – these rights weren't earned by us.

They were gifted to us by countless people who came before us and fought for democracy, for a better civil society, for civil rights and for the right to be Americans.

It's our turn now, to stand on the ramparts of our democracy and safeguard freedom of speech, freedom of the press, the 1st, 4th and 5th amendments of the US Bill Of Rights for future generations.

In the 1980s, I remember President Ronald Reagan exhorting Mr. Gorbachev to tear down the wall. And when the wall fell, we recoiled in horror at the notion that 10% of the East German population was directly or indirectly spying for the East German Police, the Stasi. I remember news pundits, politicians and talking heads saying that such a gross violation of human rights could never occur in America. And yet today, 90% of Americans spy on each other using Zuckerberg's Facebook.

If a foreign nation dared to spy on Americans as much as Facebook, Google, Apple or Amazon do, we'd declare war and launch cruise

Please send your feedback, comments and ideas to me at raj@brainlink.com

missiles. But since the surveillance state is primarily being built by US-based corporations, we somehow think it's OK.

The amount of data we let corporations collect, in the new, digital gilded age, is legal, lucrative, and against what it used to mean to be American. Either we need to change what it means to be American or we need to rein in the digital surveillance state.

You may be thinking to yourself, "but what can I do? I have bills to pay, kids to raise and a never ending to-do list at work."

First, take heart – you are NOT alone.

The Electronic Frontier Foundation (EFF) is a progressive organization that fights for the user; fights for our privacy and civil rights for the cyber user.

Privacy activists, such as, Edward Snowden and Cory Doctorow, are the new Ralph Nader.

Glenn Greenwald and Laura Pointras may as well be the new Mark Twain and ultimately, you and I have the honor and privilege of being in the crowd, marching on Washington DC, writing to our elected officials, talking to fellow parents, teachers, Boy & Girl Scout troops and anyone else who will listen that

OUR **CHILDREN** MATTER.

OUR **DEMOCRACY** MATTERS.

THE **BILL OF RIGHTS** MATTERS.

It's time to rein in surveillance, the digital police state and demand sanity, not just temporary safety.

As Benjamin Franklin said "Those who would give up essential Liberty to purchase a little temporary Safety deserve neither Liberty nor Safety.

Let's not give up our freedom of speech, freedom of individual thought, or our children's right to be kids just because some bureaucrat thinks it's dangerous.

Technology has transformed our homes, schools and workplaces, from castles to virtual prisons. Let's band together and declare that our homes and work places are sacrosanct, safe from the prying eyes of the government, petty tyrants and dotcom billionaires.

Please send your feedback, comments and ideas to me at raj@brainlink.com

Preface:
A BRIEF HISTORY OF PROPERTY RIGHTS

> *For my friends, anything. For my enemies, the law.*
> OSCAR BENAVIDES, FORMER PERUVIAN PRESIDENT

- *1215* – Magna Carta – King John stripped of divine right

- *1628* – Sir Edward Coke establishes "A man's home is his castle" in English common law

- *1791* – US Bill of Rights, 4th Amendment protects citizens from "unreasonable search and seizure"

Please send your feedback, comments and ideas to me at raj@brainlink.com

Protect Your
HOME
AND
Family

Please send your feedback, comments and ideas to me at raj@brainlink.com

CHAPTER 1

PARENTING RESPONSIBLY IN THE
Internet Era

> *Arguing that you don't care about privacy because you have nothing to hide is no different than saying you don't care about free speech because you have nothing to say.*
>
> ANONYMOUS

Data never goes away. Don't forget about that. Just because you're not using it, it doesn't mean it goes away. It will never get deleted. It's just like real life. There's stuff you and I did in high school which we hope our friends have all forgotten. At some point the record's out there but luckily for us we're old enough that a lot of this is not photographed, time stamped, and logged somewhere for the kids today. The 10 year old's, the 12 year old's, the 15 year old's, the high school kids. Everything they're doing is being photographed and indexed online. If they put a stupid photo on Facebook, or on a dating site, a kid in high school today admits to you, "Hey, I'm smoking marijuana, head banging, or doing something else." I'm sure we all did something like that in high school. We've all forgotten about it. The kids today don't have that luxury and this will haunt them for the rest of their careers until they either have a right to be forgotten online, or we socially accept that what you did then is completely forgiven.

One of the earliest cases goes back by 10 years. Back when MySpace was still around. Remember my MySpace? And Facebook was the new kid on the block. There were 2 or 3 stories which caught my attention. One of them was this nearly perfect Harvard student, 4.0 GPA, honors, all that at Harvard law. He was applying to internships in New York at the White Shoe law firms, and he got turned down for every one of them. Why? Academically he was brilliant and gifted; his MySpace profile had this scrawny little white kid from the burbs talking about "smoking blunts and talking to bitches." That was one of the first cases where a social media profile was used to deny a job to a kid. Another was about a 20 year old intern working at a printing company in Seattle, Washington,

Please send your feedback, comments and ideas to me at raj@brainlink.com

near Microsoft's campus. He was working for the printing agency that did all the printing of Microsoft's marketing materials. He took a photo of a truck full of Mac G5's being offloaded, put it up on his personal homepage for the blogs, and he wrote, "Even the evil empire uses G5's." Within 24 hours, not only was his internship terminated, his employer lost a multi-decade contract with Microsoft because one of their interns had leaked data that Microsoft didn't want to make public.

This comes down to good parenting and using common sense. As a father of two girls, in our house social media is completely forbidden. My kids don't have their own email accounts. They are not authorized to go on social media, LinkedIn, Facebook, anything like that. And the rule in my house is my kids will get their own social media accounts when I can trust them with the family car, when I think they're old enough to drive. **And the mistake I see a lot of people making is confusing the hot new technology, the cool thing everybody else is doing with good parenting. Just because everybody else is doing it, it doesn't mean your kids should be doing it. And just because it's technically feasible it doesn't mean it's a good idea.**

I remember when I had my kids, surely we are all proud to be parents to our kids. I don't recall posting the due date online. But today there are sites that will encourage parents, grandparents, whoever else to put up their baby bump photos, the prospective date of birth, etc. Parents, grandparents think nothing of publishing online: "My new baby daughter born today named Sophia Rose, date of birth, weight, city, state, parents' names..." and you have just permanently destroyed your child's right to privacy for life. We know the name, date of birth, city of birth, mother's maiden name, what else do we need to open a credit account in the child's name? Social security number? That's pretty easy to get in your local social security office. This is the real threat we see, just because it's cool, just because you can put up the "we're having a baby" website it doesn't mean you should. Just because you can put up "we're expecting our baby on July 15th" it doesn't mean you should. This is the mistake people are making with technology, people are saying technology is different. It's a tool and in most cases it's actually your enemy.

Use common sense. Teach your kids about social media, teach yourself about social media. The internet is no different than teaching your kids or yourself how to cross the street. We weren't born knowing to look both

16

ways, somebody had to teach us that. Use common sense, think before you post. And if you never ever want to explain it to your grandmother or the judge in court don't put it online.

RELATED CONTENT:

What to teach your kids webinar. *http://www.brainlink.com/what-to-teach-your-kids-employees-and-interns-about-social-media/*

Action Items:

- *Watch the video above.*

- *Watch it with the kids, interns and grandparents in your life.*

- *Share it with your PTA, Boy/Girl Scout troop, teachers, school principals, etc.*

Please send your feedback, comments and ideas to me at raj@brainlink.com

CHAPTER 2

HAS SOCIAL MEDIA GONE UNSUPERVISED
For Far Too Long?

> *Time tested internet security principle: assume anything and everything you do on the net is discoverable by someone (and this someone is likely to be the worst case for you when it happens).*
>
> ANONYMOUS

Dangers of Social Media: Responsible Parenting

Most do not realize it, but sharing too much information on the Internet -and in particular social media - presents a real and serious danger. Maintaining personal privacy is vital in order to avoid becoming a statistic. The social media generation does not seem to share these same fears, nor does it have the filters of private vs. public.

Social media concerns fall into two distinct areas: The fact that nothing on the Internet will be deleted, and companies mining information about users in order to market to them. Professionals in the industry point out that 16-year-old students who share nude pictures of themselves across the Internet are just as likely to be branded sexual predators as adults. Many are clueless as to the severity of these actions.

Here is a point to consider, "there are district attorneys in this country who have jailed kids and have labeled them sexual predators for life even when they were in a consensual relationship with each other with parental approval. So now they're branded as sexual predators for life. They will be barred from certain jobs. They will not be allowed to live in most neighborhoods, and Joe Average really doesn't distinguish between two kids who are stupid at 16, sending naked pictures of themselves to each other and a 40-year-old creep who rapes little girls."

This issue is not going away. ID theft is on the rise, and public records are moving to online storage. This means that anyone can find information

Please send your feedback, comments and ideas to me at raj@brainlink.com

about potential marks. Posting personal and private information online can result in unintended and serious consequences as evidenced by the above, and this is only the beginning of the problem.

Most of the youth of today think they are bulletproof and immune because they are online. This is not the case, as evidenced by the number of 'cyber detectives' who specialize in finding and prosecuting those who would download, post or view child pornography. It is a serious crime, and most children do not understand this. Being branded as a sexual predator is a stigma that will remain with someone for the rest of their lives, and the ramifications are severe.

While this is important, there are other aspects of social media and privacy that many people do not understand and never consider. One of the least understood examples - metadata - is another topic that people need to know about and to be concerned about with regards to their personal safety and privacy. A good example is a person who has been laid off from a job.

Now that this person is laid off, they go home and post this information on social media. Soon, red flags begin to pop up. Questions like, "Why were they fired? Is the business going under? Does my company need to continue working with this company?" Suddenly, there is a wildfire from a small spark.

Posting too much information on social media can result in thieves triangulating your location in order to commit the perfect robbery. Posting one thing on Twitter, another on Facebook and yet another on LinkedIn can lead thieves to your door at the most opportune time to rob you completely blind, and you are left clueless as to how it happened.

One of the best possible ways around this problem is to enact laws similar to Canada and Europe, where companies must have permission to use any personal information and data, but the U.S. does not have this particular law. This is why credit bureaus are so frequently targeted for attacks, and why it takes such a long time to rectify the situation.

Email is another area that many do not understand, and this lack of understanding goes beyond those of the social media generation. According to the 1986 Electronic Communication Privacy Act, emails more than six months old do not require a subpoena for access. This means that Google/Yahoo/Microsoft routinely provide information to the government.

The solution is to be smart with what you do and the way in which you do it.

Training children to use technology wisely is no different than teaching them to drive. Start with the basics and move forward. Maturity is the key to proper online behavior.

Young people need to learn about the dangers of sending sexually explicit pictures to one another and the ramifications of being labeled a sexual predator for life. The use of computers and technology needs to fall under similar laws and guidelines to driving.

Parents discuss the basics of driving, perhaps even while driving themselves, then the young driver takes the wheel, slowly working his/her way up to more and more driving within varied situations. Finally, the young driver has acquired the skills for independent driving.

Lawn Darts To Hot or Not

Every form of addiction is bad, no matter whether the narcotic be
alcohol or morphine or idealism.

CARL JUNG

On July 4, 2015, the New York Times published an article titled "Teenager's Jailing Brings a Call to Fix Sex Offender Registries" (http://www.nytimes.com/2015/07/05/us/teenagers-jailing-brings-a-call-to-fix-sex-offender-registries.html). It tells the story of Zachary Anderson – a 19-year old college student, now branded a "sex offender" by the Michigan penal code.

What was his crime? He used an app called "**Hot or Not**" to meet a girl. Both of them used Hot or Not to meet each other, both of them consented to have sex in a nearby park. According to both families, the

Please send your feedback, comments and ideas to me at raj@brainlink.com

girl lied about her age (she was 14, not the 17 year old she claimed to be) and both families asked for leniency in Zachary's case.

The law, and the presiding judge, however, did not take either the circumstances or pleas from both families into account.

The girl testified in court:

"I don't want him to be a sex offender, because he really is not," the mother said, according to court transcripts. Her daughter told the judge that she felt "nothing should happen to Zach," adding, "If you feel like something should, I feel like the lowest thing possible."

The judge in the case however, was not swayed, and he remarked:

"You went online, to use a fisherman's expression, trolling for women, to meet and have sex with," he said. "That seems to be part of our culture now. Meet, hook up, have sex, sayonara. Totally inappropriate behavior. There is no excuse for this whatsoever." – Judge Wiley

Did Zach break the law by having sex with a 14-year old? Yes.

Did he knowingly break the law? Not according to the transcripts

And yet, his career as a promising Computer Science student has been destroyed. The terms of his probation require him to **"stop using the Internet for five years".**

Imagine that.

No email. No Google. No Smartphones. No Skype. No Facebook. No Netflix. No Wikipedia.

Could you, your family or your business survive that?

Most of us couldn't. But that did NOT stop the State Senator from Michigan, Mr. Rick Jones from commenting:

"There are lots of jobs that don't involve computers," he said. "There are all sorts of trades. Truck drivers, welding. There are other opportunities." – Rick Jones, State Senator

So, what does all this have to do with Lawn Darts?

There used to be a game called "Lawn Darts" and as its name implies, it was a family game where you threw large metal darts at a target on the lawn.

Sounds harmless…and for the most part, it was. As long as it was used by responsible, sober adults.

In the hands of children however, it posed a safety hazard.

In the 1970s, the US banned the sale of lawn darts. Toy manufacturers sued and got the ban modified. Lawn darts could be sold, as long as they weren't marketed as toys.

(hmm…tell me if you see a slippery, legal fudge here…)

In 1987, seven-year-old Michelle Snow was killed in Riverside, CA when she was hit by a lawn dart thrown by her brother's friend.

Between 1980 & 1988, 6,100 people were injured by lawn darts. 81% were 15 or younger. 50% were 10 or younger.

Michelle Snow's dad, David Snow channeled his loss into leading a lobbying campaign that led to the full ban of Lawn Darts in 1988.

The question for you, dear reader, is how many teen lives will we see destroyed before we declare that dating and hookup apps that do not properly age-verify users are no different than digital lawn darts?

How many years will we sit by the sidelines while a generation gets locked up for using tools meant for adults, but built with ZERO safety, NO age verification and HIDDEN behind weaselly EULAs and "Terms Of Service"?

Drunk Drivers, Amateur Porn & Twitter

Twitter is one of those dangerous toys that if it gets in the hands of the wrong person, you'll have the mind of a 12-year-old masquerading as an adult.

COLIN QUINN

Please send your feedback, comments and ideas to me at raj@brainlink.com

Bars, Pubs and bartenders have existed as long as humanity has.

And so have drunks.

With the invention of automobiles, so have drunk drivers.

In every state of the union, we have "Dramshop Liability Laws" – these laws prohibit bars from selling alcohol to minors and hold bar tenders legally liable if they sell alcohol to inebriated or drunk patrons.

> *Considering that "impaired drivers" cause one-third of the traffic fatalities (over 12,000 a year), and also considering the fact that alcohol related crimes are estimated to cost over $200 billion a year, it's a wonder that states have not criminalized the act of serving alcohol to inebriated patrons.*
>
> *Actually, they have.*
>
> *According to a 2009 NHTSA study prepared by the Pacific Institute for Research and Evaluation (PIRE), nearly every state and the District of Columbia prohibit sales to intoxicated people (known as SIP laws). However, there is considerable variation among state laws both in terms of language employed to describe intoxication as well in defining what it means to "provide" alcohol. Further complicating things is the fact that states vary as to the level of proof required to prove guilt as well as who can be held liable for a violation of a SIP law.*
>
> *Rich Stim, Attorney*

http://dui.drivinglaws.org/resources/dui-and-dwi/can-bartender-arrested-serving. htm

In a documentary called "Hot Girls Wanted", Actress Rashida Jones ("The Office", "Parks and Recreation") explored how twitter and social media is used to groom and recruit young girls to work in the amateur porn industry.

A really disturbing piece in the documentary is where young girls show how they use Twitter to post revealing photos, and how adult porn producers use Twitter and Craigslist to recruit and exploit these girls.

At which point do we hold Twitter liable for these girls getting exploited? What makes Twitter so pernicious is that it allows/encourages kids as young as 13 to get Twitter accounts; and Twitter does not have a policy or technical mechanisms to prohibit posting pornographic materials.

As an adult, I accept that adults have the right to drink; the right to smoke; the right to watch porn (or not); the right to use Twitter (or not).

As a parent, and a citizen, I also agree that bars should not serve liquor to minors; and shops shouldn't sell cigarettes or tobacco to minors.

As a society, we took on RJR Reynolds, Joe Camel, and the entire tobacco industry. We forced them to stop marketing cigarettes to kids; and we required the tobacco firms to pay for anti-smoking campaigns.

Isn't it time we required Twitter (and others) to actively prevent young girls (and boys) from posting nude or semi-nude photos and videos online?

Isn't it time we required the social media giants, and the cell phone carriers to fund, produce and deliver EFFECTIVE anti-sexting and anti-underage-sex campaigns?

Action Items:

- *Think of computers as cars. Would you let your child drive without training or a license?*

- *Treat ALL email as postcards – assume that everything you have written can be read by others.*

- *Talk to your kids about what they are doing online.*

- *Be their parent, not just their friend.*

- *Don't adopt new technology until you or they understand the social and legal consequences.*

- *Just because it's new or cool does NOT make it necessary, or safe.*

Please send your feedback, comments and ideas to me at raj@brainlink.com

- *Read http://www.nytimes.com/2015/07/05/us/ teenagers-jailing-brings-a-call-to-fix-sex-offender-registries.html*

- *Read http://www.nytimes.com/2010/03/21/ us/21sexting.html*

- *Use EFF's DEMOCRACY.IO site (https://democracy. io) to contact your congressional representatives and demand that app makers be held to the same standards as lawn darts manufacturers.*

- *Read http://dui.drivinglaws.org/resources/dui-and-dwi/can-bartender-arrested-serving.htm*

- *Read http://www.alllaw.com/articles/nolo/auto-accident/dram-shop-laws.html*

- *Read http://news.yahoo.com/rashida-jones-talks-amateur-porn-industry-documentary-with-katie-couric-203552949.html*

- *Watch "Hot Girls Wanted" on Netflix - https://www. netflix.com/title/80038162*

CHAPTER 3

Grandparents
ARE OFFERING THEIR GRANDKIDS TO PREDATORS

> *Loose lips sink ships. Uploaded photos sink grandkids.*
>
> ANONYMOUS

A lot of people are going to read that and say that could never happen to their children or grandparents.

Yet, it is true. Grandparents who are on social media do love to post pictures of their grandchildren. It's what grandparents do. They are proud of their grandkids and want the world to know it.

But, who is looking at those pictures other than close friends and family? Facebook in particular gives friends of friends permission to see any post where the first generation of friends makes a post.

Let's put that another way.

Grandma posts pictures of grandchildren. It's a birthday party. Grandma only allows friends to post on her page. She links to her friend Margaret. Margaret sees the post and makes a comment.

Margaret doesn't have the same security protocols.

Margaret's friends can see the post as well. Margaret, through no fault of her own, has approved a predator on her friends list. It could be a friend approved to earn benefits in a Facebook game. But now, this predator has information about Grandma's grandchildren, including everything she posted about the children.

Names

Ages

Addresses

Parents

Please send your feedback, comments and ideas to me at raj@brainlink.com

That's enough for someone who steals identity to make fake accounts in the grandchild's name. It not just fake social media accounts. With a few keystrokes, the thief can set up fraudulent online shopping accounts and expand from there into more financial fraud.

Grandma has set up her grandchildren for a lifetime of identity fraud issues. She never meant to do this, but it still happened.

Action Items:

- *Educate the grandparents in your life – do NOT post family photos online. Yes, it's easy, but it's extremely dangerous. You're better off sending grandma a small printed photo album – she'll appreciate that more.*

- *Teach grandparents to use Facetime and let them spend some realtime with your kids.*

CHAPTER 4

PREVENT YOUR KIDS FROM
Spending Thousands
ON IN-APP PURCHASES

> *If you want your children to turn out well, spend twice as much time with them, and half as much money.*
>
> ABIGAIL VAN BUREN

Yes, I agree, the iPad/iPhone/Smartphone is the new babysitter & nanny.

We all want our kids to do better at school, pick up technical skills, be excellent digital natives…and really, we want them out of our hair for just a few minutes while we decompress, or recover from the insanity of the day.

Here's an excellent way to preserve your sanity AND your bank balance. Update the device settings to DISABLE or CONTROL IN-APP purchases.

CHECK DEVICE SETTINGS

Before you hand your kid the smart device, check settings – does it allow in-app settings? Can it be disabled?

ANDROID:

1. Open **Google PLAY** app

2. Find **Settings**

3. Select **Require Authentication for purchases**

4. Enter your **PIN or Google password**

5. **Require authentication for EVERY purchase**

6. **Do NOT share this password with your kids!!!**

7. **Test the App – confirm that you or your kids cannot bankrupt you thru in-app purchases**

Please send your feedback, comments and ideas to me at *raj@brainlink.com*

Also see: http://www.littlegreenrobot.co.uk/tutorials/how-to-disable-in-app-purchases-on-android/

IPHONE/IPAD/IOS:

1. Go to **Settings -> General -> Restrictions**

2. **Enable** Restrictions

3. Enter your **PIN CODE**

4. **Prevent in-app purchases**

5. **Test the App – confirm that you or your kids cannot bankrupt you thru in-app purchases**

Also see: *https://support.apple.com/en-us/HT204396*

Action Items:

- *Read http://www.cultofmac.com/236589/apple-refunds-8-year-olds-6131-bill-for-inapp-purchases/*

- *Read http://www.cnet.com/news/apple-refunds-8-year-olds-4000-bill-for-in-apppurchases/*

- *Read http://www.cultofmac.com/233013/if-your-kids-racked-up-a-huge-bill-in-in-apppurchases-apple-is-ready-to-make-amends/*

CHAPTER 5

The Fine Line
BETWEEN GUIDANCE AND SURVEILLANCE

> *Hey teacher, leave them kids alone.*
>
> PINK FLOYD, THE WALL

'In Loco Parentis' Increasingly Means Schools are Crazy

Courts have long held that when a child goes to a school, school officials serve as in loco parentis. This essentially means the school staff takes over some of the responsibilities of a parent.

With the advances in technology and the ability to monitor students away from school, some educational systems are taking the in loco parentis entirely too far. A report in the Technology section of the New York Times said some companies are offering school systems the ability to search networks to see what kids are doing outside of and away from school.

As outrageous as this sounds, it is a reaction to a number of teenage suicides. These children killed themselves after suffering from online bullying.

It's not the school system's responsibility to monitor what children do outside school. That is a job for the real parent (or guardian).

The other problem that arises with this tremendous invasion of a student's privacy rights is the security behind these systems. Schools which gather this information and collate it also store much more sensitive information about children, up to and including medical records and Social Security numbers.

A cyber criminal breaking into a school system's network has immediate access to hundreds to thousands of student records. That's valuable

Please send your feedback, comments and ideas to me at raj@brainlink.com

information in today's black market information world.

One of these "security" companies is Safe Outlook Corporation. Company president David Jones told CNN, "You can identify a student, and you can jump into their activity logs and see exactly what they've typed, exactly where they've gone, exactly what they've done, and it gives you some history that you can go back to that child and use some disciplinary action."

How long will it be before someone uses this kind of information for malicious purposes instead of helping students? History tells us, not long. It may have already happened and we just don't know about it.

As a parent, what can you do? Ask what information your child's school stores electronically. Ask to have as much of it removed as possible and emphatically say your child's non-school activities may not be monitored.

RELATED RESOURCES AND REFERENCES:

- **New York parents furious at program, inBloom ($100M, funded by Gates, Murdoch, etc), that compiles private student information for companies that contract with it to create teaching tools**
  http://www.nydailynews.com/new-york/student-data-compiling-system-outrages-article-1.1287990

- **School pays $70K to student forced to give up Facebook password**
  http://www.nydailynews.com/news/national/school-pays-70-000-forcing-student-reveal-facebook-password-article-1.1736528

- **Principal creates fake account to spy on students**
  http://www.cnet.com/news/principal-resigns-amid-accusations-of-facebook-spying

Keeping an Eye on the Kids: A Culture of Surveillance

Behave... The Internet Never Forgets.

JAMI GOLD

In today's world, headlines abound with reports of violence, harassment, and other threats in our schools. As a result, the safety of our children has become an ever-increasing concern, and society as whole has embraced increased surveillance of students. While our intentions may be good, the unfortunate consequence is that we treat our children in schools, at least in America, worse than prisoners in a prison. Our kids in schools have less civil rights than prisoners do.

Kids in schools don't have freedom of speech. In a lot of schools, they don't have freedom of dress. They are getting RFID tags put on them. We're training our kids to grow up as prisoners. They have no freedom of movement, congregation, or speech.

So what are we training them for? When they graduate school, go to college, and graduate college, what mindset are they bringing to the table? It's not unreasonable to conclude that this generation will feel surveillance is okay. They won't mind having their every movement tracked. In fact, our cell phones are already doing that for us right now.

How, then, can we expect our children to defend their own privacy when we are conditioning them to surrender it? In working to protect our kids, we must be sure we are not infringing on the same right to privacy that we expect for ourselves.

Action Items:

- *Ask your school for their social media and digital learning policies – and READ them. Don't let legalese and hand-waving fool you. If you don't understand it, ask them to clarify.*

- *If your school district offers you free ipads or laptops, ask them "what's the catch"*

- *Don't believe the eLearning hype – ipads, tablets and computers are NOT the best learning tools for all kids. Despite all this technology, I don't foresee*

Please send your feedback, comments and ideas to me at raj@brainlink.com

paper textbooks, pen or paper becoming extinct anytime soon.

- *Teach your gradeschool kids to NEVER friend teachers, principals, etc. (what they do in college is completely different).*

- *Read the US Constitution and the Bill Of Rights.*

- *Remind yourself of your constitutional rights*

- *Teach your kids their constitutional rights.*

- *(YOU remember having to memorize and recite the Bill Of Rights? Or the nifty video on School House Rock?)*

Right to
PRIVACY
IN THE
21st Century

Please send your feedback, comments and ideas to me at raj@brainlink.com

CHAPTER 6

THE RIGHT TO
Digital Privacy

> *After executing family members, the #KGB used to send a bill for the bullet; today, we pay phone bills that subsidize our own surveillance.*
>
> CORY DOCTOROW

The Fight for Privacy

For those of us older than Millennials, we grew up in the age of privacy. We all learned at some point that loose lips sink ships; don't say anything you wouldn't say or repeat in public. Our kids and grandkids have no such training. People share what they had for breakfast and "like" what the girls are wearing at school. They feel every moment in life needs to be shot through a tiny, little screen to be posted online.

How many of you have gone to concerts and have seen people glued to their cell phones shooting a concert they paid 80 bucks to see? I actually admire musicians who go, "Turn the damn things off or I'm going off-stage. Watch the performance, and buy the recording later."

For those of you who think about social media and privacy and are concerned about it and about what to teach the young people in your life, there are some things you might want to know and arm yourself with. Every legal system, no matter where you are in the world, says ignorance is not a defense. And if you choose to be an ignorant about social media, computing, and digital privacy, you can't say, "I didn't know. No one told me." You have to educate yourself.

Eric Schmidt, the CEO of **Google**, once said, **"We know where you are, we know where you've been, we more or less know what you're thinking about."** When people have questioned the invasion of privacy from technology like Google Street View, he has responded, "If you have something you don't want anyone to know, maybe you shouldn't be doing it in the first place."

Please send your feedback, comments and ideas to me at raj@brainlink.com

Surprisingly, more recently he had this to say: **"You have to fight for your privacy or you will lose it."** How is the man who helped shepherd a company that is the largest violator of privacy suddenly privacy's champion? What happened in his professional life that now he says we have to fight for privacy? Oh, could it be because drones are now commercially available, and he doesn't want his neighbors flying drones over his property? Either way, the sentiment is true.

We, as consumers, parents, and users, must educate ourselves on the ways burgeoning technology affects our personal lives, and we need to speak out against corporations and government policies that abuse that technology. We must be actively demanding our right to privacy, or we will lose it.

Consumer Rights in Cyber Space: The Need for Safeguarding Our Privacy

Freedom is never more than one generation away from extinction. We didn't pass it to our children in the bloodstream. It must be fought for, protected, and handed on for them to do the same.

RONALD REAGAN

Our country has a wonderful history of citizens standing together and demanding rights owed to us. The auto manufacturers in America, for example, fought every single safety innovation, including seatbelts, anti-lock brakes, and airbags. They were willing to let people endanger themselves with their cars and faulty tires until Ralph Nader and other consumer rights activists banded together and said, "Enough is enough." We saved billions of lives globally by insisting on better, safer cars.

The same thing applies in the realm of social technology. We need user rights. We need the rights that we have enforced, and we need new protections under new technologies. You and I are alive today because writers and social activists got together and demanded that the government police food. As a result, the FDA was established within the last century to enforce our right to health. Users need an equivalent for digital rights, civil rights, and cyber rights for the 21st century. And no one's going to give it to us. We ourselves have to demand these rights, demand these controls. Otherwise, who else will protect our right to privacy and that of technology users for generations to come?

In the real world, if a kid commits a crime except for a couple of heinous things, the records are sealed. The records are sealed for life unless the kid becomes an adult and does something else. That forces the cops on the opposing side to have those records be unsealed later in life. In the civil and legal world, we have a legal amnesia for minors. That is not true on the internet. That's not true electronically. We need to have the digital amnesia rights. We need a new conversation on civil rights for minors and adults in cyber space.

I'm not saying no to technology. I am a gadget freak. I love new tech. That's why I'm in technology. But, I am saying that as responsible, adult citizens in our countries, we need to locally and globally demand that user rights protections be built into the architecture. Everything from 'give me the ability to verify all the information Facebook has on me' to 'give me the ability to permanently delete my LinkedIn profile if I choose to'. There's no corporation as strong as the consumer. No government is as strong as the American consumer. And what we need to do as other countries have done is we as adults need to get together and actually demand our rights. More important, we need to go back to the Constitution, read it again, read the Declaration of Independence, and be the check and balance on government and on corporations. That's our job. Our job is to raise our kids, take care of our communities, and at the end of the day, leave this place better than we found it.

Action Items:

- *Think before you post, click or take a selfie*

- *ENJOY the movie, concert, book, meal, etc. Let someone else Instagram/tweet/post it.*

- *Support the EFF (www.eff.org)*

Please send your feedback, comments and ideas to me at raj@brainlink.com

- *Educate yourself on your constitutional rights AND CIVIC responsibilities. Ask yourself, are you an engaged citizen or a mindless consumer? The former have rights – the latter are products and victims.*

CHAPTER 7

The Paradox
OF NOT OWNING WHAT YOU BUY

> *Surveillance is a kind of power and counter-surveillance*
> *is an act of resistance.*
>
> LAURA POITRAS

Big Brother Wants His Book Back: The Realities Of Digital Rights Management

I love reading books, and as an informed consumer I either buy paper books or I buy eBooks. But, I do not buy Kindle books. Why? I prefer to buy eBooks from publishers that give me eBooks without the DRM (digital rights management) because I don't want them to know what books I've read. I don't want them to be able to track what page I'm on, what paragraph I'm reading, and I don't want them to delete or take back what I bought because they don't think I should be reading it. Amazon, they make billions selling Kindles and conveniently—or humorously enough—the first book Amazon revoked for people who paid for it was 1984. Somebody bought a Kindle in the States, bought 1984, they went back to a European country that Amazon didn't have the right to sell eBooks in. So without telling the consumer, they went to Kindle and deleted the book, no refund, no nothing. That's not a one-time event. In the US they went and deleted books from high school and college students. Not only did the students lose the books, they lost all their notes. I love eBooks, I have hundreds of them. But, I only buy them from publishers and stores that don't think they have the right to know what I read, and to revoke my purchases. But when you rent books from Amazon, or music from Amazon or Apple, you're not actually buying anything on iTunes, you're merely renting it, and they have the right to revoke the purchase any time they want.

Remember what happened when Apple rolled out the new iPhone 6 with free U2? They didn't ask if you wanted a U2 album; they gave it to you automatically. I don't mind getting a free gift, I don't mind getting music,

Please send your feedback, comments and ideas to me at raj@brainlink.com

and I happen to like U2, but I absolutely object to a company deciding voluntarily to do something with my data or my account without a notice or with my permission. As a consumer, don't hesitate to do your research and take a stand when companies' policies do not respect your rights and privacy.

GM, John Deere: You don't own your car or tractor, they do

> Nowadays in the digital world you can hardly own anything anymore, if you put things in the cloud, someone, somewhere might disappear and it's gone forever. When we grew up, ownership was what made America different than Russia.

STEVE WOZNIAK, APPLE CO-FOUNDER

It's no secret that cars, tractors, refrigerators, TVs, toasters, everything is getting smarter due to software. Software turns dumb appliances into smarter, more useful or convenient gadgets.

What manufacturers don't tell you is that the old-school car/truck/tractor/washing machines have quietly become software companies... and they own the code running in the gadgets you bought.

Recently, farmers tried to repair their tractors (as farmers have done for decades) and John Deere prevented them from servicing equipment they had spent $100,000-$500,000 for.

As John Deere said in their filing with the copyright office:

"...farmers don't own their tractors. Because computer code snakes through the DNA of modern tractors, farmers receive "an implied license for the life of the vehicle to operate the vehicle."
http://www.wired.com/2015/04/dmca-ownership-john-deere/

GM and other auto manufacturers joined the lawsuit in favor of John Deere, and against us, the consumers.

Here's what GM submitted in their legal brief:

> *"Proponents incorrectly conflate ownership of a vehicle with ownership of the underlying computer software in a vehicle.... Although we currently consider ownership of vehicle software instead of wireless handset software, the law's ambiguity similarly renders it impossible for Proponents to establish that vehicle owners own the software in their vehicles (or even own a copy of the software rather than have a license), particularly where the law has not changed."*

https://www.techdirt.com/articles/20150421/23581430744/gm-says-that-while-you-may-own-your-car-it-owns-software-it-thanks-to-copyright.shtml

Welcome to rentier capitalism where you don't own things that you "buy", you merely lease it.

Action Items:

- *Separate your online purchases into 2 categories – PURCHASES and RENTALS.*

- *I "rent" movies and TV shows from Netflix. If they disappear, I will survive.*

- *Musicians I care about, I buy their CDs from Amazon, and then legally download MP3s from Amazon.*

- *Books and novels that I like are bought as paper books.*

- *Ebooks are bought from stores and authors that do not embed DRM. I disable wifi on my ebook reader unless I'm actively downloading books or surfing the web.*

Please send your feedback, comments and ideas to me at raj@brainlink.com

CHAPTER 8

The Myth Of
Online Privacy

> *You can't download a patch for human stupidity.*
>
> KEVIN MITNICK

Social Media: The Myth Of A Private Profile

Typically the biggest problem social media companies face is the issue of privacy—or rather how to reassure their consumer that privacy is a priority. They all have privacy policies; Facebook, Mark Zuckerberg says "we value your privacy". Eric Schmidt says he values your privacy. All of these companies say we value your privacy, but do they really? You could believe the terms of service, you could believe what the manufacturer says. Personally, I prefer believing what the courts and lawyers tell me.

In the UK, someone who worked for Apple stores went on Facebook and posted on his profile rude comments and complaints about his manager. One of his Facebook friends printed out the comments, and gave it to the manager. The guy got fired. He sued, citing the EU Human Rights Act. He said, "They violated my privacy, invaded my privacy." And at the UK tribunal, more than one judge ruled anything on social media is not private. Therefore, those privacy settings are a lie. The UK is not alone; AU and the US also have rules that say if your minors are involved, media can't publish names or photos unless they were approved from parents or third parties involved. A TV show went to a kid's Facebook page, grabbed some photos and ran a news story with it. Parents sued for violation of privacy. The AU media regulator ruled that if it's on Facebook, it's public domain. The truth is that a "private" profile is anything but.

Learning All Your Secrets? There's an App for That

Mass surveillance creates 'data time machine so you can go to any moment & reconstruct a person's data identity.'

@KATECRAWFORD

Like any software, apps have problems; but that's just the given nature of software. For a privacy law expert, apps present a very interesting civil and privacy rights argument. Any app store owner – whether it's Apple with their iTunes store, Amazon with their Amazon store, or any other similar entity – not only knows what you bought, but they know down to the word you're reading. What's the last word you heard on an audio book? What page are you reading? What are you reading? That data is in Apple's database and Amazon's database.

At some point, all these databases are going to talk to each other because they want to share this data freely. Netflix just spent a fortune getting the video privacy law revoked. And why do they care? If you rent a video, the video store can't tell anybody what you rented, which is fine in the physical world but Netflix isn't like that. They want to be able for you to tell people on Facebook what movie you're watching, what you're downloading right now. They spent the last couple of years lobbying Congress and now, if you rent a DVD from Netflix, they can't tell the world what you rent. But if you rent the same movie as a streaming video, they now have the legal right to encourage you to share on social media about this cool TV show you're watching. And when I rent a DVD, Netflix doesn't know whether I even watched it. When I stream a video on the other hand, Netflix knows when I watched it, how far I got into it, how many times I watched it, what scenes I am fast-forwarding to, and what scenes I skipped.

The result is all of this data is being collected and at some point, it's going to be harvested in ways that designers never imagined. In some cases, the uses are benign and useful. In other cases, it's not benign but it's legal. The real challenge, the real threat, is the law of unintended consequences. We have no idea what's going to happen when the things that are collected today become analyzable, and that's why we should do our best to be informed and careful with the products we use and the data we share.

Action Items:

- *Read Chapter 13: The Real Cost Of Facebook*

- *Discuss it with the people in your life*

- *Understand your social media usage, settings, etc. and make informed choices.*

- *Delete unused apps.*

- *Before you download an app, ask yourself, ""Do I really need this?"*

- *Where possible, don't start the bad habits in the first place. Yes, I'm actively advocating cyberluddism.*

Please send your feedback, comments and ideas to me at raj@brainlink.com

CHAPTER 9

INFORMATION TO THE
Highest Bidder:
THE DATA EXCHANGE BETWEEN
GOVERNMENT AND PRIVATE BUSINESS

> *Every dystopian society has excessive surveillance, but now we see
> even western democracies like the US and England moving that way.*
>
> PHIL ZIMMERMAN, CREATOR OF PGP
> (PRETTY GOOD PRIVACY)

It's well understood that the government cannot ask you, "Who do you sleep with? What do you smoke? What do you drink? What are your political views?" But did you know that any information held in a commercial database can be bought by the government? As more and more private corporations collect data from their customers, we as the consumers face having our personal information sold without our knowledge. Private companies are doing things for their own benefit that in the long run will come back to haunt us.

One example? Realistically it is impossible for a police department to drive around and see every license plate, and run a license plate check on them. But separately, a couple of repo men have built massive databases where they pay investigators to drive around. All these cars do is photograph every single license plate, put them in databases, and do a database check. But a couple of them are now turning around and selling this data to private companies and to government for a pretty penny. So where the government can't legally go around photographing every single car, they can buy it. And they are. So I'm not saying the repo company had no right to collect this data. They have the right. We allow it. But there's no control of what they can do with this data or what control we have as citizens.

Right after 9/11 a private corporation had one of the largest databases in

Please send your feedback, comments and ideas to me at raj@brainlink.com

the country. They went through all of their data to find information on potential terrorists. They gave the FBI 30 names with their full profiles. Four or five of the hijackers ended up being on this list. Within a week, his company got a very nice contract, a couple hundred million dollars to provide these profiles to the FBI. Legally, the FBI cannot get this data from us. They can't ask for this data unless we are actually being investigated, but they can buy it wholesale because it's available for commercial purchase.

When OnStar came out, GM sold it because it was a great, life-saving tool. You're in an emergency, press the button, and they'll call the emergency responders for you. If your keys are locked, they can unlock your car. If you lock your kid in your car, they can unlock it for you. And when OnStar came out 10, 12 years ago, no one really thought about the privacy aspect of OnStar. Then last year, OnStar admitted publically when they updated their terms of service that by being an OnStar subscriber in the past or now, you've given them the right and the permission to sell your data to third parties.

These are only a few examples of a growing trend, and they all highlight the need for better consumer protection laws. Private corporations and government are not evil entities, but consumers should be able to know what is being collected from them and how it is being used.

Action Items:

- *Keep an eye on what your vendors are doing.*

- *Where possible, vote with your dollars and do business with companies that respect your privacy.*

CHAPTER 10

Invasion Of Privacy:
IS IT THE USER'S FAULT?

> *The User's going to pick dancing pigs over security every time.*
>
> BRUCE SCHNEIER

It's always the user's fault, isn't it? "You clicked on that link. You must have gone somewhere." Don't we always blame the users?

But it's not always the user's fault. In legal circles there's a concept called **"attractive nuisance"**. If you had a pool in your backyard without a proper fence, and your neighbor's kids come over and drown in it, you are liable. If you've got a playground in your yard and you don't have signs and you don't keep your neighbor's kids out, if they come in and break their neck on your trampoline, you are legally liable.

Eric Schmidt, a man who works for the biggest data mining company on the planet, said in an interview, "Street view cars, they only drive by a home once a year. You can move can't you?" So apparently the solution to keep your privacy out of the Street View is that you've got to move. Because moving is so easy isn't it? Don't you just love moving on a regular basis? How is the average person – by staying in their own private home – to blame for having their place of living put on display for the whole world?

Not long ago Mark Zuckerberg's sister tweeted a photo, likely by accident. The media cropped the photo and published it. And Randi Zuckerberg, Mark's sister, had this to say when she complained of this photo being published, "It's not about privacy settings; it's about human decency." Ironic? Maybe she should take her little brother to task for violating human decency, because Facebook's privacy settings aren't considered private whatsoever. And yet as much as corporations might want to say that the consumer is to blame for sharing their private life online, the fact is that the creator of Facebook's own family feels that it's not entirely the user's fault.

Please send your feedback, comments and ideas to me at raj@brainlink.com

Action Items:

- *GM spent billions of dollars fixing a manufacturing defect. Johnson & Johnson spent millions of dollars changing HOW they package medication after the Tylenol poisoning scare. Why did GM & J&J spend billions of dollars? Because CONSUMER PROTECTION LAWS demand that these manufacturers sell good that are free from defects or safe for human consumption.*

- *Ask yourself why are Microsoft, Adobe, Facebook, Amazon, Apple, JPM Chase, etc allowed to get away with losing your data? Why are they allowed to be cavalier with your private details? Because they don't get to cleanup the mess they created.*

- *It's time to stop treating software companies like they are special form of manufacturing and demand LEMON LAWS FOR SOFTWARE. I'm happy to pay for my own stupidity – I don't see why you should have to pay for their laziness or stupidity.*

- *As Malcolm Gladwell in BLINK pointed out, we don't have safer, fire-resistant houses because contractors and home builders became enlightened. We have better buildings because insurance companies demanded better building standards.*

- *We don't have safer cars because GM, FORD or TOYOTA are do-good charities, We have fantastically safe and comfortable cars because the IIHS tests cars every year and rates them on a Five-star scale for safety.*

- *When was the last time your software came with a trusted, independent PRIVACY SAFETY rating?*

- *Demand more from your vendors, legislators and yourself.*

CHAPTER 11

Ad Blockers
MAKE THE WEB SAFER AND FASTER!

> *If someone is treating you as the enemy, then maybe you are.*
>
> JOHN MCAFEE

Have you ever used TiVO or another DVR to skip commercials? Doesn't that make TV watching bearable?

Or are you a Netflix-junkie who adores the freedom of watching TV shows and movies without ads?

Wouldn't it be great if you could TiVO the internet? Well, you can...and the rewards are incredible.

1. Install AD Blockers in your browser.
   - Ad Block Plus is a great add-on for Firefox and Chrome

2. Enable Firefox Tracking protection.
   - Type **about:config** in Firefox's browser bar
   - Search for **privacy.trackingprotection.enabled**
   - Double-click it to enable

3. Implement managed firewalls at work (and/or home) that block internet ads.

Why would you want to do all this?

As a recent research paper by Georgios Kontaxis and Monica Chew shows "Firefox's Tracking Protection feature improves page load time on average by 44%. In addition, it reduced the average data usage when connecting to the top 200 Alexa websites by 39%, and dropped the number if HTTP cookies by 67,5% on those sites"

http://www.ghacks.net/2015/05/24/firefox-tracking-protection-decreases-page-load-times-by-44/

Please send your feedback, comments and ideas to me at raj@brainlink.com

The
BANES
OF
Technology

Please send your feedback, comments and ideas to me at raj@brainlink.com

CHAPTER 12

Lessons Learned
FROM CENTCOM, CRAYOLA AND ISIS HACKERS

> *Passwords are like underpants. Don't let others see them, change them regularly and don't loan them out to stranger.*
>
> UNKNOWN

A few months before this book was published, pro-ISIS hackers broke into the YouTube and Twitter accounts for US CENTCOM and sent embarrassing tweets and videos. During the same weekend, another group of criminals hijacked the Crayola Facebook account and sent lewd/adult photos to embarrass Crayola.

You can watch my interview with WPIX11 here:

http://www.brainlink.com/about-us/media/pro-isis-hackers-take-control-of-us-central-command-twitter-account/

So what lessons can you learn from these (and other) incidents?

1. Criminals, joy riders, competition and ex-employees will take any opportunity to embarrass you.

2. You have to manage your social media accounts appropriately.

3. You have to have a fallback plan for when (not if) your social media accounts get hijacked.

Appropriate social media account management:

1. You have to know who in your organization has social media accounts that your company relies on

2. Preferably, these accounts are not tied to that individuals' personal identity.

Please send your feedback, comments and ideas to me at raj@brainlink.com

3. For example, it's far better if your twitter account is owned by marketing@yourcompany.com versus being owned by happyjane123@Gmail.com

4. You must enable two factor authentication for your social media accounts

Treat your social media accounts as you would corporate credit cards. Each one of these allows the user to trade on your personal and corporate reputation. Hopefully, your CFO is not as cavalier about handing out corporate credit cards as many of you are with letting anyone sign up on social media as your company's global marketing representative.

The US CENTCOM has a massive budget, a very strong security posture, and yet they made a rookie mistake. It seems that their twitter and YouTube accounts were both controlled by the same username and password and had not enabled two factor authentication on these accounts.

Crayola is a large corporation, and a brand we've cherished from our childhoods. They too made the unavoidable mistake of not enabling two factor authentication on the Facebook account and as a result faced global embarrassment and getting defaced.

As I mentioned in my WPIX11 interview, you have to assume that your social media will get vandalized. You may recall in the 1980s, graffiti artists took great pleasure in spray painting graffiti on other people's properties. Today's graffiti artists don't use spray paints to deface your property and your reputation, they use a keyboard.

And while it may not be fair to you to pay for the cleanup caused by these vandals, as a business owner it is up to you to safeguard your property, protect your reputation and have a fallback plan for when you do get defaced.

READ MORE:

http://www.adweek.com/adfreak/crayolas-facebook-page-got-hacked-and-oh-my-look-color-posts-162300

Two very important lessons to learn from both these attacks are:

1. **Have a plan for recovery** - US CENTCOM jumped on the issue rapidly, communicated with the press effectively to gain control of their account quickly.

2. **You can't wait for customers to complain** - Crayola was a bit more flat-footed and it took them much longer to get their account back in control.

Action Items:

1. Identify who in your firm uses social media on your company's behalf.

2. Document those username and passwords.

3. Move the access from personal accounts to company-owned accounts.

4. Make a plan for speaking with the media when you're accounts get defaced.

5. Enable 2 factor authentication on your accounts.

Please send your feedback, comments and ideas to me at raj@brainlink.com

CHAPTER 13

THE REAL COST OF
Facebook

> *Vanity. It's my favorite sin.*
>
> AL PACINO, THE DEVIL'S ADVOCATE

Facebook can assist in Home Invasions

What does Facebook ask you to do? Friend your friends, neighbors, businesses, restaurants, your neighbor's dog or anything else with a pulse.

And in the sleepy city of Nashua, NH, a burglary ring did just that – they friended all their neighbors and strangers who lived in or around Nashua.

And this clever (or lazy!) group of criminals kept track of who had bought a new TV, expensive jewelry, fancy TVs, etc. And when the homeowners went away on vacation, the criminals broke into 50+ houses and stole $100,000+.

And what great technology did these criminals use to target their victims? The Facebook location update.

REFERENCE:

http://gawker.com/5635046/real+life-burglary-ring-uses-facebook-to-choose-victims

Facebook can cause Unemployment

> *The Age Of Privacy is Over.*
>
> MARK ZUCKERBERG

Please send your feedback, comments and ideas to me at raj@brainlink.com

In 2011, Mr. Crisp worked at an Apple Retail store in the UK. He posted negative comments about Apple on his Facebook page and marked them PRIVATE. One of his so-called "Facebook friends" printed the comments and gave them to Crisp's manager. After reading the comments, the manager summarily fired Mr. Crisp from the Apple store.

Mr. Crisp sued Apple for violating his rights under the **European Convention on Human Rights.** (side note: I love the case name "**Crisp vs Apple**"!)

After reviewing the case, the tribunal rejected Mr. Crisp's arguments for reinstatement.

On what grounds did Crisp lose to Apple?

1. As part of his employment, Crisp had signed the Apple Social Media policy. From the Tribunal's proceedings, "Apple had in place a clear social media policy and stressed in their induction process that commentary on Apple products, or critical remarks about the brand were strictly prohibited".

2. Despite having "private" Facebook settings, the tribunal decided that there was nothing to prevent friends from copying and passing on Crisp's comments, so he was unable to rely on the right to privacy contained in Article 8 of the European Convention on Human Rights (covered in the UK by the Human Rights Act 1998).

3. He retained his right to freedom of expression under Article 10, but Apple successfully argued that it was justified and proportionate to limit this right in order to protect its commercial reputation against potentially damaging posts.

Facebook can hurt your Credit Rating

If you have something that you don't want anyone to know maybe you shouldn't be doing it in the first place.

ERIC SCHMIDT, CEO, GOOGLE

You know those deadbeat friends of yours on Facebook? They could end up killing your credit score and costing you a loan. At the very least, your no-account pals could bump up your interest rate.

Most banks have plans to analyze your social media profiles to determine how big a credit risk you are. It's yet more evidence that, **unlike Las Vegas, what happens on Facebook doesn't stay on Facebook** – and could come back to bite you in unexpected and unpleasant ways.

How are banks going to use this information? First, they're going to use your friends list to troll for future prospects. If you just took out a line of credit against the equity in your house, maybe your friends will too – assuming they've got any equity left.

It gets worse. Let's say you fall a few months behind on your payments and you've decided to banish the bill collecting goons to voice mail. Hong Kong-based micro-lender Lenddo – which asks for your Facebook, Twitter, Gmail, Yahoo, and Windows Live logons when you sign up — reserves the right to rat you out to all your friends.

READ MORE:

http://www.pcworld.com/article/246511/how_facebook_can_hurt_your_credit_rating.html

Facebook can lead to Jail Time

> *Being evil while telling everyone else not to be ... is how big business makes big profits, and it is more apple pie American than selling snake oil and claiming it is an elixir. Whatever Google is selling, all of us paid dearly for free.*
>
> ANONYMOUS

In 2009, two American tourists, Vanessa Palm and Daniel Rust took a trip to the Bahamas. During their trip, they illegally captured, butchered, cooked and ate an iguana.

As reported on Metro.co.uk, capturing, killing or eating iguanas is against the law as "iguanas are protected under the Convention on International Trade in Endangered Species of Wild Fauna and Flora" (CITES).

Please send your feedback, comments and ideas to me at raj@brainlink.com

To make matters worse, the couple posted photos of their iguana barbecue on Facebook.

In Feb 2015, an Australian tourist to Abu Dhabi took what she thought was a "funny" photo of a car that was parked across two disabled parking spaces, without displaying the handicapped permit. She then posted the photos on Facebook.

In the US or UK, these might be considered funny photos, and might even serve as a meme.

In Abu Dhabi, however, posting that photo made her guilty of "writing bad words on social media about a person" – and that is illegal under Abu Dhabi law.

As a proponent of Free Speech, I support your right to speak your mind.

However, you MUST remember (and teach your kids!) that what is legal or funny at home may be illegal or dangerous abroad.

Action Items:

- *Disable LOCATION updates on Facebook, iPhone, iPad, Android and any other app that demands to know your location.*

- *Keep GPS off until you need it*

- *Uninstall unnecessary apps (because most apps ask for permission to access your contacts, GPS, email, etc).*

- *Assume everything you post, link, like or tweet is public.*

- *Never disparage employers, vendors, employees, teachers, students or neighbors online.*

- *Teach your kids good manners – "If you can't say it to their face, then don't say it online"*

- *Or better yet "Don't say anything online. Period."*

- *Be wary of any credit, loan or cash offers that require your social media credentials.*

- *Do NOT like or friend your lenders (after all, when was the last time your bank or mortgage company treated you as a friend?)*

- *Have a discussion about "Social Media pros and cons" before you travel to foreign countries*

- *Read articles and news stories about what is, and isn't, permitted on social media in those countries*

- *Ensure you have your local Consulate or Embassy's contact info handy. You never know when you'll need the US State Department or your Foreign Office to get you out of jail.*

Please send your feedback, comments and ideas to me at raj@brainlink.com

CHAPTER 14

HOW YOU SPEND YOUR TIME ONLINE
Can Be Used Against You

> *We know where you are. We know where you've been. We can more or less know what you're thinking about.*
>
> ERIC SCHMIDT, CEO, GOOGLE

According to the American Academy of Matrimonial Lawyers, 81% have used or faced evidence from Facebook, MySpace, World Of Warcraft (WOW), Twitter, LinkedIn, etc.

See: *http://kotaku.com/5576262/farmville-world-of-warcraft-are-divorce-lawyers-latest-weapons-in-court*

and

http://www.usatoday.com/tech/news/2010-06-29-facebook-divorce_N.htm

For example:

1. A father seeking custody of his kids claimed (among other things) that his ex-wife neglected their young ones. Subpoenaed evidence from the gaming site World of Warcraft tracked the mother online with her boyfriend at the precise time she was supposed to be out with the children.

2. A mom denied in court that she smokes marijuana but had posted partying, pot-smoking photos of herself on Facebook.

Action Items:

*   *Always assume that online games are tracking your location and can be used against you in court.*

Please send your feedback, comments and ideas to me at raj@brainlink.com

- *You are much better off playing offline games (e.g. I prefer to play Diablo 2 vs Diablo 3; Command & Conquer Generals vs C&C Online; Real Scrabble with my kids vs Words with Friends; My phone has zero games; I do not engage in online, real-time video gaming with friends – for real-time gaming, I prefer Cards Against Humanity (CAH), Poker or Settlers Of Catan).*

CHAPTER 15

ADULT FRIEND FINDER DATA BREACH
- *Blackmail R Us?*

> *An ounce of prevention is worth a pound of cure.*
>
> BENJAMIN FRANKLIN

Whether it's Tinder, Snapchat, AshleyMadison or AdultFriendFinder (AFF), many people aren't looking for love...they're looking for instant physical gratification. There's nothing wrong with sex between consenting adults.

However, there's plenty wrong with submitting your sexual preferences online.

To quote from the **International Business Times:**

> *Blackmail*
>
> *The information contained in the leak includes usernames, post codes, emails, dates of birth, and even the unique internet addresses of users. It also includes details of which forums most interest the users (subporno, BDSM) and could easily be used to carry out spear phishing attacks against users or potentially blackmail campaigns.*
>
> *Ken Westin, a senior security analyst at Tripwire, highlighted the problems.*
>
> *"The Internet has essentially become a database of You. As more data is breached, this information can be sold in underground markets and can create a very vivid profile of an individual," said Westin.*
>
> *http://www.ibtimes.co.uk/adult-friendfinder-hack-reveals-user-preferences-bdsm-pornography-having-affairs-1502513*

Like everything else in life, you have a choice.

Please send your feedback, comments and ideas to me at raj@brainlink.com

You can think about the risks, make prudent choices and minimize the disruptions to your personal and business life…or you can submit your peccadillos to websites and apps…and hope your future spouse/employer/law enforcer doesn't find out.

Action Items:

- *If you are going to engage in online dating or adult sites, then learn how to cover your tracks.*

- *Do NOT use your regular work or personal email addresses.*

- *Do NOT use your home or work computers.*

- *Do NOT use your work or personal phone.*

- *Buy a disposable, throwaway phone, tablet and/or laptop.*

- *Or better yet, just watch the free stuff at home or learn how to meet partners in real life.*

CHAPTER 16

WELCOME TO THE AGE OF
Online Dating

> *Love may be blind...online, it is also exceedingly gullible.*
>
> ANONYMOUS

Internet Love Often Ends in Fraud

According to a recent article in New York Magazine:

People looking for love online were the worst-hit victims of internet scams in the U.S. last year. The FBI's annual online-fraud report found that people who reported being victims of romance scams were swindled out of a total of $82,315,378 — which comes out to a staggering average of about $14,000 each. These costly schemes often involve scammers mining dating sites and social media for personal information to initiate online relationships with their targets (in 70 percent of cases, women over the age of 40), and then inventing hardships like family tragedies or extreme life circumstances to ask for money.

Catfish R Us - How to avoid getting baited

> *The bad guys don't have to be smart, they can use something that's 7-8 years old.*
>
> STUART ASTON,
> CHIEF SECURITY ADVISOR AT MICROSOFT UK

These days, more and more people are being deceived by Internet users who use false online personas in order to lure out their victims. Many of you may be familiar with the television program CATFISH on the MTV network, or the famous incident with Mante Te'o, the Notre Dame football star, who is probably most well known for his now false girlfriend, an example of the catfishing phenomenon.

71

Please send your feedback, comments and ideas to me at raj@brainlink.com

The world of online dating has exploded, and there are plenty of documented cases of people finding and settling down with a successful relationship. However, for every one good case, there are likely thousands of scammers and frauds trolling these sites looking for lonely and desperate people.

It's a fast-growing industry. From my perspective as a security researcher, user rights activist, and somebody who works with corporations around New York City to help them address their security and privacy threats, dating sites are a great way to go and get data on people that you won't get otherwise.

Many professionals have two or more social media pages. LinkedIn, for example, is normally sterile and bland. It focuses on the professional side of a person, talking more about their professional work and behaviors. However, if you were to search up the same person on a dating site, you may realize that you can't always judge someone by their social media profile.

When you go to these dating sites, you learn so many things about these people, including stuff that they probably never even revealed on Facebook. What they like to drink, their sexual activities, restaurants, you get a complete profile of the person. It is here that real problems can occur. Now, a potential predator, scheme artist or blackmailer can get private information simply because the account owner is providing such a wealth of personal information. Worst of all, the information will never go away, even if the account is closed from non-payment.

This is only the beginning. 10-15 years ago there were only one or two sites. Now thousands of dating sites claim tens of millions of members, and this is an underestimate. The average dating site user signs up on one to five dating sites, but in reality your data can appear on several hundred to several thousand dating sites around the world.

Each new dating site buys, steals or trades data and information to create a false portfolio of members. This way, the site is more enticing to potential users. The steady stream of late night infomercials about the sites promises the millions of members, all looking for a date, relationship and possibly marriage.

The real danger of dating sites is the information put on the site, and the way that information can be publicized. If you update something on one site, Match for example and only as an example, a user makes a note of a preference of hot tea. Later on, it is changed from hot tea to coffee.

Many times, the information put on dating sites is not the innocent choice of hot beverages, but information that is much more sexual in nature. This is compounded by the fact that information shows no lack of restraint. It may seem little to nothing, but the clone sites that hack this information put users in the perfect position for being highly compromised.

This is nothing new. Dating sites have simply applied the exploiting schemes used in mail orders on the back of magazines to the Internet. The Internet has only changed the way people can scam others, and the number of people that can be scammed at any one time. Exceptionally good scammers can have several on the hook at any one time on multiple accounts even on the same site.

The real problem for security stems from the way people will not delete their data, or the dating site's TOS (terms of service) make removing data virtually impossible. Often buried well into the fine points is a disclaimer that all information posted becomes the property of the site. Julian Assange is an excellent example of someone who has carefully covered themselves online. When Assange was doing WikiLeaks, you couldn't find much about him online because he had led a very, very clean low profile except for leaking the data, or helping to publish leaked data. When the media did find something, it turned out to be nothing more than a catfish.

FINAL THOUGHTS

There is nothing wrong with using a dating site, but keep the information clean and sterile. Concentrate on normal likes such as movies, church activities, outdoor activities, music choices and the like. Save the explicit for the privacy of one-on-one companionship.

Please send your feedback, comments and ideas to me at raj@brainlink.com

Action Items:

Repeat after me:

- *There is NO Nigerian prince willing to share his inheritance with me.*

- *There are NO Russian (or Chinese, Thai, Indian, British, etc.) men or women desperate to meet me.*

- *The number of attractive, single people online is less than the number of attractive, single people at my local bar, Applebees, Synagogue or Church Social.*

- *Caveat Emptor (Let the buyer beware) and remember a fool and his money are soon parted.*

- *Want a date? Forget the apps and sites.*

- *Ask your friends; attend events at local museums, dog parks, wine tasting evenings, etc.*

- *No app, no online test can match you for compatibility, sense of humor, cute smiles or sheer, chemical excitement.*

- *Simply put, Marilyn Monroe didn't need eHarmony or Facebook...neither do you.*

CHAPTER 17

SOCIAL SECURITY IS
Not Secure

> *Social security, bank account, and credit card numbers aren't just data. In the wrong hands they can wipe out someone's life savings, wreck their credit and cause financial ruin.*
>
> MELISSA BEAN

1936, Congress created the social security number, a national ID number meant only to be used by the IRS for reflecting income taxes. That's actual official law.

In 1938, a wallet manufacturer's vice president of marketing produced an imitation of the social security card, using his secretary's social security number, and placed a copy in every wallet made with the newly patented plastic pocket window. Starting in 1939 and continuing through the years, 40,000 people filed their taxes using that secretary's social security number. Even forty years later, 1977, 12 people had still filed their taxes with this same number. It is funny, but here's the punch line: the fact is that to this day only the IRS are allowed to use SSN numbers for any identifiers. Your banks are not supposed to use them, your insurance companies, your credit card companies, your mortgage companies, your schools, your universities – they're all violating federal law. Try getting a loan or a job without an SSN number; they're becoming the de facto ID number.

And why is this a problem? Let's compare your social security number to your credit card number. You have a credit card, and if you lose it, you call your bank. How fast do they cancel the number? In about a minute. You get your new card in a couple of days. If I'm a merchant and you give me your credit card, how fast can I tell if it's yours and if it's active or not, or if you have enough money in the account? Thirty seconds or less and I can validate if it's yours. I can actually verify your identity and your bank balance, or at least your fund limit, with a single charge.

Please send your feedback, comments and ideas to me at raj@brainlink.com

But with social security numbers, the story is different. How many of you can tell me absolutely no one else in the country has your number? How many of you can check your SSN number and know you're checking the right person? You can't. The SSN number pool is too small - the SSNs are reused/recycled. We used to have two different people, one dead, one living, with the same SSN number. To this day, you can't validate it, you can't repudiate it. And yet they've become the de facto ID card for our country.

What happens when somebody's ID gets stolen – who pays the bill for the clean up? Is it the thief, is it the companies who benefited, or is it the poor consumer who will spend thousands of hours and thousands of dollars trying to get their life back?

Action Items:

- *Demand that 3rd party data brokers be held liable for breaches.*

- *If your social security number is to be used for identity verification purposes, demand that the government establishes more security protocols.*

CHAPTER 18

Beware
THE SMART HOME OF THE FUTURE

> *We have invited Mossad/NSA in to our living rooms, and happily pay for the privilege. #kinect #smartTVs #pointcloud #facetracking*
>
> HAGBARD CELINE

Smart House is an Oxymoron

The stories made headlines for days. A hacker broke into the system new parents were using to monitor their baby remotely.

When the parents got into the room, the remotely controlled camera was pointed at them, not the baby. The cyber attacker screamed obscenities and so on at the parents and baby.

Reacting as expected, the parents pulled the plug on the monitoring system. Foscam monitoring equipment was used. The company announced and posted a patch to make the systems more secure, but as of this spring, an unknown number of Foscam systems were still being used without the patch, according to an article in Forbes magazine.

The article concludes with a statement from from staff writer Kashmir Hill: "As we increasingly bring Internet-connected devices into our homes and workplaces, we have more devices that can be hacked if they are not properly designed."

Properly designed or not, networked devices are subject to being hacked.

The idea of a hacked baby monitor is disturbing. Other devices that are subject to cyber attack can lead to life threatening problems. Cars with controls that can be operated remotely is just one of these problems. Joshua Corman of I Am The Cavalry told Forbes: "If my PC is hit by a cyber-attack, it is a nuisance; if my car is attacked, it could kill me."

Take this a step further. Remotely controlled insulin pumps have been hacked. The Forbes report discusses a conference in England where a

Please send your feedback, comments and ideas to me at raj@brainlink.com

researcher demonstrated this in a successful attack. Again, a potential for murder and thanks to the way the security protocols on these devices are rigged, the murderer would likely never be caught.

It may be that you're not worried about those kinds of attacks because you don't have Internet-controlled devices. Really? How to do you get online from home? A US cyber security firm found 300,000 compromised routers in homes around the world. In 2012, a group of cyber criminals from Brazil successfully attacked 4.5 million routers and gained access to bank accounts.

In what is likely a true story whether or not this instance really happened, one Internet user got a divorce and lost the house he and his ex wife bought together. Before separating, they installed Smart controls on the heating and AC. After the divorce, the ex and her new husband did not change passwords for HVAC access. The former husband said he took great delight in freezing the couple and driving temperatures to South Texas levels.

if you want a really Smart house, do not install Internet controls on the most important devices and make sure your router has firewall protection and hard-to-break passwords.

If you want a picture of the future, imagine a Roomba leaking pix of your home, forever

If you have nothing to hide you won't mind if we install webcams that we control in your bedroom and bathroom.

DAN GILMOUR

Cory Doctorow Mon, May 25, 2015

The game-plan for future Roombas may fit them with cameras that send images of your home to a remote service that identifies obstacles and lets the little robots clean around them -- what could possibly go wrong?

Roombas will be equipped with standard cameras. They will use standardized operating systems -- probably a stripped down GNU/Linux or BSD variant. Their network and USB firmware will come from the same factories that produce the components in your laptop. They will connect to the same home router that your phone and computers and set-top boxes use. The images will encrypted with the same crypto that everyone else uses. The servers that receive those images will be regulated by the same laws that regulate the servers that store instant messages, emails, and social media postings.

Each one of those components is under assault today.

The FBI and David Cameron have vowed to ban strong crypto. GCHQ and the NSA sabotage cryptographic protocols by sneaking saboteurs into standards bodies and using them to argue for the deliberate weakening of random number generators.

The Snooper's Charter will require service operators to retain the images they receive, and grant warrantless acess to law enforcement, government officials, and any crook or tabloid reporter who can bribe, trick or coerce a cop or a baby into leaking the password.

GCHQ and the NSA know about vulnerabilities in USB ports and other standardized components, but they keep these a secret, most likely so that they can weaponize them).

Please send your feedback, comments and ideas to me at raj@brainlink.com

Roombas are pretty useful devices. I own two of them. They do have real trouble with obstacles, though. Putting a camera on them so that they can use the smarts of the network to navigate our homes and offices is a plausible solution to this problem.

But a camera-equipped networked robot that free-ranges around your home is a serious threat if it isn't secure. It's a gift to everyone who wants to use cameras to attack you, from voyeur sextortionist creeps to burglars to foreign spies and dirty cops.

Irobot is the first major company to propose using roving cameras to solve an appliance problem, but they won't be the last. Your home of the future will be stuffed full of cameras, some of which will be able to see through your clothes and your walls. Those Internet of Things videos where people dressed like extras from Tron use gestures to control their homes? Those are depicting houses where every square inch is under video surveillance.

Cybersecurity starts with defense. We can't make back doors that only good guys can walk through. Our spies and spooks and militaries can't make us secure by eroding our security. If we backdoor these things to help SWAT teams executing no-knock warrants, we'll leave them open to revenge-porn scum, the Syrian military, and corporate espionage contractors, too.

Roombas already can detect and avoid objects, but recognizing exactly what those objects are is a different beast entirely. By streaming video from its cameras to a cloud-based object-classification system, it can tell whether the object in front of it is a bookcase or a TV stand, label it accordingly on a map, and share that detailed plan with next-generation home-infrastructure systems.

The camera system wouldn't be the only modification necessary for the Roomba to create maps of your home. Because iRobot's map-making system uses the cloud to analyze, recognize, and label objects, connectivity would need to be built into the robot itself or its charging dock.

"It's a camera and cloud-based AI engine where we trained it on faucets by going on the Web, downloading pictures of faucets, and using neural network learning on what makes a faucet," Angle explains. "I think it's pretty cool that it can actually differentiate dishwashers from ovens because ovens have windows in the door and dishwashers don't."

This article was originally published by Cory Doctorow. It is reprinted with his permission. I am grateful to him for allowing me to share his wisdom with you.

- RAJ

THE ORIGINAL ARTICLE IS AVAILABLE AT:

http://boingboing.net/2015/05/25/if-you-want-a-picture-of-a-fut.html

Action Items:

- **Do NOT install NEST thermostats, DROPCAMS, SMART TVs or most of the Smart House gadgetry.**

- **Seriously, just say NO.**

- **Your life worked fine before you were able to lock/unlock doors from your iPhone. Kids were raised for THOUSANDS OF YEARS without baby monitors.**

- **Your life will be a LOT better, happier and richer if you stop becoming a new gadget freak.**

- **Ask yourself – do YOU want spies in your bedroom, bathroom or kitchen? All the smart TVs, smart watches, fitbits, smart thermostats are tiny little spies reporting to the mothership. You would be MUCH better off spending that cash on a nice cruise, trip to Europe or reading paper books.**

Please send your feedback, comments and ideas to me at raj@brainlink.com

PUBLISHED
Articles

Please send your feedback, comments and ideas to me at *raj@brainlink.com*

Beware The Little Sisters

By Wil Thijssen, Photo by An-Sofie Kesteleyn

This article originally appeared in De Volkskrant - *http://www.volkskrant.nl/vk/nl/2844/ Archief/archief/article/detail/3394833/2013/ 02/16/Vrees-de-Little-Sisters.dhtml*

Everybody spies on everybody on the Internet. Your blogs, emails, tweets and Photos can [and will] always and everywhere be used against you ICT expert Raj Goel warns. He fights for privacy and self-determination rights of the computer user.

Raj Goel
Founder of Brainlink

Founded in 1991 Brainlink, a Consultancy for companies in the field of advantages and disadvantages of ICT.

He was also manager for the Internet Services of Market Guide, a division of The News Agency Reuters. Goel speaks regularly at cyber conferences on the dangers of social media

On New Years day a young man from Colorado wrote on Facebook: "Jesus, I was so drunk last night. Sorry to the person whose car I grazed tonight. "Five minutes later one of his Facebook Friends called the police, the same day the man was arrested for driving by after a collision."

Another example. An American man who had translated a Thai book into English on Facebook, was arrested when he visited his family in Bangkok. The book was critical about the Thai king and according to Thai law prohibited. The offer of the police: if you say that you are guilty, then you only get a few years in prison, if you plead innocent then we lock you up for 20 years. The man is now sentenced for of 2.5 years cell.

All his Facebook Friends who could read the translations, are guilty of "lese-majeste" according to the Thai law. They can forget a holiday in Thailand.

"Of course it's good as a drunk driver is arrested after a collision, "says ICT expert Raj Goel. "But what people do not realize is that your blogs, emails, tweets and photos can be used as evidence against you. And messages that are acceptable in a western Democracy may be punishable in other countries. Internet has no boundaries."

Goel fights as a missionary for awareness and the lack of human rights in the cyber world. He speaks on international conferences, such as recently in The Hague. His children, 9 and 11 years, can only use email under his supervision and may not use social media . "As long as I don't trust them with the the car keys, they are not allowed to go on the digital highway without parental supervision. If your children do have permission", he says, "make sure that they are aware of the dangers."

Criminals

In the 'normal' world the record of a minor won't haunt him his whole life.

A 16-year-old American boy who had sex with his girlfriend, shortly before her 16th birthday, and wrote about it on Facebook, was arrested and sentenced. He is now branded as a 'pedophile' and 'sexual predator' for the rest of his life. The internet does not forget.

A woman found it out the hard way – she was seeking custody of her children. She said in court that she never used drugs. The lawyer and her ex found photos of her through social media where she smoked hash [marijuana]. She was sentenced - not because of the hash - but because of perjury. The children live with her ex-husband now.

Photo's can be used against you in various ways. What most computer users are unaware of, says Goel, is that shooting with a Smartphone which the GPS is turned on - which is almost always the case - not only reveals when and what time a picture

is taken, but also where. The wife of John Sawer, head of the British Secret Intelligence Service MI-6, three years ago had shared pictures of her family on Facebook during a holiday in Southern France. Facebook Friends could not only admire the Sawers in their swimsuit, but through the metadata in the digital photos also their - location . The result: bodyguards in the pictures had to be replaced, friends in the photographs had to be provided with British government paid security. This fiasco has cost the UK government millions of euros.

Security Strategy

The children of Michael Dell, the owner of Dell Computers, had uploaded pictures of their holiday in Fiji on their social media pages. This way the address of this wealthy family was easy to track. Their security efforts, for which Dell, Inc. paid $ 2.7 million per year, immediately became worthless.

Another computer magnate, John McAfee, founder of the anti-virus software company, got arrested in Guatemala in early January. He was a fugitive for several months, under suspicion that he killed his neighbor in Belize. The journalist who interviewed McAfee in Guatemala, published pictures of him on his website. [The metadata in the photos was not redacted] within a day the police knocked on the door of McAfee's hiding place.

"If these computer moguls and their

Please send your feedback, comments and ideas to me at raj@brainlinx.com

children are making these stupid mistakes", says Raj Goel, "how can you and I protect our children? Do they know the risks of their online behavior?" Goel cites the example of police officers in Wisconsin that are spending time on the Internet disguised as a beautiful young woman. The "beauty" is trying to be friends on Facebook with as many young people as possible. Once pictures are detected of the minors drinking alcohol (that's what I read in an article), they are fined $227 by the police for underage drinking and may get a criminal record.

The New York City Police Department discovered in the computer of a pedophile the complete profile of a 12-yearold girl in Pennsylvania, hundreds of miles away. Through the internet, he knew her friends, classmates, hobbies, pet, cheerleading team and favorite clothing brand. Under a false name, he had friended the girl and her school friends. "He knew more about her than her parents and teachers," says Goel. According to investigators, the man had planned to kidnap and abuse the 12-year-old. He very accurately mapped the route she traveled to and from school and all her stops along that route and at what time she made those stops. "He knew all this without ever being near her".

"The smartphone is the best spying tool ever invented"

A survey of American educational facilities by Kaplan showed that profiles on social media sometimes affect the admission of young people to schools. This includes contacts with friends and relations. Several admissions committees admitted that they sometimes have refused students on the grounds of their social media profile. The same applies to managers, they look increasingly on LinkedIn and Facebook in equal candidates for a job. "You have a clean profile," says Goel, "but if your internet friends are unsavory, they may choose some other applicant."

Goel finds it unacceptable that many rights that are guaranteed in the physical world, lack on the Internet. He wants to unleash a new struggle for human rights, but now for the cyber world.

A struggle for privacy rights, copyright and especially the self-determination of the computer user.

Why do companies collect your data? And why are they preserved for eternity?

"Collectively, all of us have built one large jail cell around the world," says Goel. "And the smartphone is the best spying tool ever invented." About thirty thousand times per month a mobile phone tells a provider where a phone is located. Because the device is usually in the pocket or handbag's owner, the provider can determine within a meter's accuracy which routes a consumer takes. Data stored in databases remains forever.

Last year the FBI was rebuffed by a court for placing GPS trackers under vehicles of suspects which according to the judge was an unauthorized invasion of privacy. Later when the FBI submitted the GPS data of the mobile phones they had acquired from the cell phone carriers, this was accepted as admissible evidence. Why? "Because you are not the owner of the location data of your phone," says Goel. "Your cell provider is the legal owner. The investigators did not even need to show a court order to recover it. Waving a badge is enough."

Love Letters

The same applied to the discovery of the love letters from former CIA Director David Petraeus in his gmail account. "If he had received the letters from his mistress through the postal mail, FBI agents would have needed a search warrant from a judge to read them. But because they were emails, the FBI didn't need court approvals to acquire the emails", says Goel.

The discovery of those letters cost Petraeus his position as head of the most powerful intelligence agency in the world.

Investigation services on the web are increasing in power. In the Netherlands the parliament discusses about giving the police permission to hack a citizens private computer. If the police should hack on computers of citizens. In Europe the Ministers of justice investigate the possibility of how a criminals server can be infiltrated that is abroad - which usually is the case -, the internet knows no boundaries – without violating the sovereignty of a country. Goel thinks that the sovereignty of the individual citizen is already violated too much.

The American Patriot Act, that came into force after the attacks on the World Trade Centre in 2001 requires each provider to hand over all data on their customers to law enforcement, without notice to their users, when asked by the FBI. The provider cannot inform their users subsequently.

Google has announced that the search engine and Gmail provider in 2012 was forced to provide the personal information of 54 thousand users (from different countries, also from the Netherlands) to investigation services. Other social media sites, like twitter, Facebook and Linked-in, and web shops like Amazon are not publishing what information they had to release. But the total information the police have gathered, will be many, many times more than the 54 thousand of Google that they admit to releasing.

Lies

"At least as bad", Goel says, "is the fact that it is almost impossible to get providers to remove incorrect information about a user from a

Please send your feedback, comments and ideas to me at raj@brainlink.com

search engine. Even if someone lies about someone else, removal requires costly litigation or other methods, usually paid for by the victim," says Goel. "It is the same as the location data from your phone; not you, but the provider is the owner of everything that's on social media." A court in New Zealand, required Google to change incorrect information about a NZ citizen, under penalty of $100,000. Google paid the fine.

The same is true for photos that Google was ordered by a judge to delete from the internet, and later still were popping up again. Without realizing it, internet users leave their fate in the hands of browsers and social media. Goel says "you have no power over your internet content." "New legislation is required that would decrease the power of Internet companies. The provider should not determine what happens with digital information - users should be able to correct or delete information from these [Facebook, Google, etc] databases".

Did the digital world become a Big Brother Society?

"It's not Big Brother, but the Little Sisters that we must fear," says Goel. "If something happens anywhere, it is published immediately via Smartphone, cameras or social media and lives online forever." "We don't live in a society where one eye watches everyone, but where billions of eyes are increasingly spying on each other. This is a kind of control that even George Orwell could not imagine."

Contacts:

Wil Thijssen
Politie- en
justitieverslaggeefster
De Volkskrant
w.thijssen@volkskrant.nl
+ 31 20-5623417
+ 31 6-55816338
www.vk.nl

Raj Goel
CTO & Co-Founder
Brainlink International, Inc.
raj@brainlink.com
917-685-7731
www.brainlink.com
www.rajgoel.com

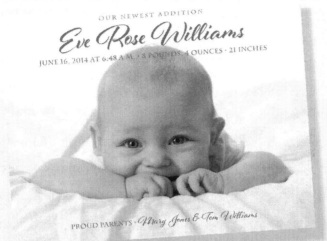

WATCH AND SEE

OUR NEWEST ADDITION

Eve Rose Williams

JUNE 16, 2014 AT 6:48 A.M. · 8 POUNDS, 4 OUNCES · 21 INCHES

PROUD PARENTS · *Mary Jones & Tom Williams*

A CYBER CIVIL RIGHTS ADVOCATE SHOWS HOW WE'VE CREATED A GENERATION OF AT-RISK YOUTH BY RAJ GOEL

Technology Has Always existed at the intersection of hope and fear. At the dawn of the Internet age, we dreamt of a world without borders or boundaries for information routed around censorship. Several decades later, we now live in a world that closely resembles the United States television series "Person of Interest," in which we are constantly under surveillance by governments, corporations, law enforcement, our neighbors, and even our family members.

Not only does this erode our expectations (and rights!) to a certain level of privacy, but the vast amounts of data gathered in the course of such omnipresent surveillance also puts us at a much higher risk of fraud and identity theft.

But some of the outrage needs to be directed inward as we, the consumers, continue to aid and abet cybercriminals through personal data paraded on social media and handily offered to mobile apps, just to name two popular practices.

So what about a child born in 2014, who enters this world without much to trace? What information

Please send your feedback, comments and ideas to me at raj@brainlink.com

do we need to conduct ID theft or potentially ruin their reputations before they've even said their first word?

Not much.

Ways Parents And Family Members Give Up The Goods

At a minimum, we need five identifiers to impersonate someone else online or over the phone:

• Mother's maiden name
• Date of birth
• City of birth
• Name
• Phone

Long before a child is born, his parents may have married and announced their nuptials a number of ways, from a formal wedding announcement in the local newspaper (with an accompanying website) to an online site that advertises an engaged couple's wedding plans, including the couple's full names, date of the marriage and location of the wedding. This is how we acquire a mother's maiden name, provided she changed it after getting married; it is not uncommon now in many countries for women to retain their maiden names for personal or professional reasons.

More and more, prospective parents are sharing "Save the Date" or "We're Expecting" announcements. This does not give us a date of birth, but an ID thief now knows around what time to monitor a feed or local newspaper for the official announcement of the arrival. And, of course, social media plays its part by having both major and minor life events (from engagements and births to posts about how a couple first met) advertised on Facebook, Google+, and other sites where stricter privacy settings are often ignored.

As soon as the baby is born, you can expect proud parents or grandparents to send out the "Welcome our Little One" cards, posts, tweets, etc. And even in the age of HIPAA, hospitals across the United States and other nations proudly share the newborn's name, date of birth, parents' names, and in some cases, names of siblings and health care practitioners involved in the delivery.

This is how we acquire the child's full name and city of birth.

Finding a household's phone number that the child eventually "inherits" is just a Google search away, thanks to the many "people finder" services that search engine algorithms seem to love.

Home Is Where The Heart Hack Is

So, is our baby safe in his/her home?

Not really. More and more, parents are turning to technology to help manage their baby's care. And most consumer-grade equipment was never designed with security in mind.

Just ask Heather and Adam Schreck of Cincinnati, Ohio, U.S.A., who were woken at midnight to a man shouting, "Wake up, baby! Wake up!" in their 10-month-old daughter's room.

Adam ran to the bedroom and found the shouts coming from a Foscam IP Camera aimed at the crib. The camera turned to face the startled father. "Then it screamed at me," Adam told a local television reporter. "Some bad things, some obscenities. So I unplugged the camera."

Most baby cams, baby monitoring systems, and other consumer devices come with either no passwords, default passwords that are never changed, or vendor-coded back doors that can never be secured.

And not every hacker makes his secret presence obvious by screaming at the occupants.

School Daze

School shootings worldwide have led more communities to implement student monitoring systems at public and private campuses to record who comes and goes from buildings or who approaches students on school grounds. Rarely, if ever, do parents balk at the increased safety measures.

But it's a different story when it comes to technologies like InBloom, a database initiative largely funded by the Bill & Melinda Gates Foundation and built by Rupert Murdoch's News Corp.

The technology, which as of last year was adopted in nine states, creates a centralized database where student records, from attendance to disciplinary to special needs, are stored. New York City parents, including the current mayor, expressed outrage upon learning that the data could be sold to private companies.

Civil rights groups took immediate legal action to try and prevent the practice of disseminating student data—a practice that also had been taking place in Colorado, Delaware, Georgia, Illinois, Kentucky, North Carolina, Massachusetts, and Louisiana by the time the New York uproar began.

In April 2014, InBloom announced it would shut down.

Word Of Mouth

Marketers know that children and teenagers are a financial goldmine. They are easily influenced by advertising that can lead to lifelong brand loyalty. And they love to tell their friends, providing the kind of peer pressure corporations—and data mining dynasties like Facebook, Google, and Twitter—love. Their choices, and choice words, leave a lasting impression— which some come to regret.

That's one reason more and more (ISC)2 members are volunteering for the (ISC)2 Foundation's Safe and Secure Online program. Companies are not necessarily going to do right

Please send your feedback, comments and ideas to me at raj@brainlink.com

by our children, so we must teach them how to protect themselves when they use Web services and interact online and across public airwaves.

Because, as we adults all know, the Internet never forgets.

To paraphrase the U.S. Justice system's Miranda rights: Everything you say can and will be used against you, by anybody, now or decades into the future.

The Trackers Are Organized

So far, we've seen how we've put our children at risk just by being social, friendly, and even caring. But the child of 2014 will inherit governments that have the ability and perhaps the desire to conduct ubiquitous surveillance that could increasingly endanger privacy rights.

It's not just the NSA-funded programs that capture emails, chats, videos, photos, file transfers, login activity, social media profiles from a variety of entities including Microsoft, Facebook, Skype, Google, PalTalk, AOL, Yahoo, YouTube, Apple, AT&T, Verizon, Sprint, etc.

There are provisions in the United States Electronic Communications Privacy Act of 1985 that allow law enforcement to acquire email older than 180 days as well as certain online data with minimal judicial effort. These efforts were augmented by the post-9/11 U.S. Patriot Act. Civil and privacy rights advocates are continually challenging this latitude on the part of the government, but the children born in 2014 will have to learn to protect themselves.

And it's not just the U.S. federal government; law enforcement agencies in cities and towns across the country are beginning to invest in "StingRay"—a technology that can mimic a cell phone tower, thereby intercepting mobile phone numbers. Warrants are not required because the device is collecting numbers,

Ways We Put Our Children at Risk for Fraud/ID Theft

infancy to teen

- Birth announcement in the local newspaper
- Birth announcement on social media
- Online "people finders" to pin down addresses, family details
- Posts on social networks

- Unsecured webcams/baby monitors
- School announcements in local newspaper or websites
- Parents' blogs
- School databases used for marketing and research

- Social media monitoring/impersonations
- GPS on mobileware
- POS technology for target marketing

not actual conversations. And police departments are keeping mum about having the technology.

The car you drive and loan to your child is no longer just a vehicle in a stream of traffic. License plate readers, traffic cameras, and other community video functions are capturing license plate data every minute. That data is collected not only by police agencies, but by data collection firms (for sale) and auto repossession companies.

Cell Me Something I Didn't Know

It could be said that the cell phone is the best spying tool ever invented, and as users, we enable it and our children are learning to do it as well. GPS tracks our every move (and our children's). Cell phone logs show who we talk to and for how long. Our kids take pictures and share them with their friends on Instagram. Our phones can record what we say. There are apps, like CrowdPilot, that will broadcast our every word.

The cell phone quickly became part of our lives, and it'll be part of the lives of children in 2014 in ways we never even considered.

What's The Game?

So why are we being spied on, and creating a world constantly under surveillance for the children of 2014? Some will claim "safety": The advantage of knowing where our

children are, avoiding getting lost, keeping track of the bad guys, etc. But for most, it's about money.

Those ubiquitous shopping mall cameras track your every move, and point of sale technology notes your every purchase, whether it's cash, debit or credit. The value to the retailer is immense: by knowing your shopping preferences and those of your children, you can be easily targeted on birthdays, anniversaries, sales of your favorite items…all because of the data you've willingly shared.

Consider this true story from Charles Duhigg's best-seller, *The Power of Habit:* retail giant Target used its proprietary data profiling service to determine that a teenaged customer in New Jersey was pregnant, based primarily on her purchase history. They began to mail her coupons for baby products and other materials for expectant mothers. The young woman's father called the store manager to complain that the mailings were inappropriate because his daughter wasn't pregnant. The store manager apologized profusely, believing the technology had malfunctioned. But a few months later, it was the father who was apologizing. Unbeknownst to him, his daughter was indeed pregnant

and later gave birth.

That incident took place several years ago. What are we to make of the technological advances since?

93

Please send your feedback, comments and ideas to me at raj@brainlink.com

Everything poses a threat, from drones hovering over neighborhoods to our neighbors hovering over their own Web cams.

The Watchers Are Everywhere

In London, our child will be photographed by the largest collection of government surveillance cameras in the world. In Russia, his/her telephone and email metadata content, as well as all Internet Wi-Fi, and social media traffic may be monitored by law enforcement.

Whether our children are at home or abroad, they are being watched—but not in the way a parent would prefer. On every continent, we live under the watchful eyes of governments, corporations, and other private entities. It is up to us as parents, citizens, and information security practitioners to help protect the most vulnerable segment of society: our children.

We cannot always compete technologically, but we can certainly do our part to spread awareness and to speak out, as parents in New York City did, when that technology goes too far and places our children in harm's way.

It's important that each of us, as information security practitioners and private citizens, teach the children and adults in our lives that no privacy rights exist on the Internet—not in Canada, the U.K., Russia, China, or even the international space station.

Welcome to the life of a child in 2014.

RAJ GOEL, CISSP, is a cyber civil rights advocate, author, and speaker who will speak about global surveillance architecture at this year's (ISC)2 Security Congress September 29 - October 2 in Atlanta.

InfoSecurity P rofessional • July/August 2014

Googling Security
and Privacy

The search giant saves a lot of information. Here's what you should know.

It's no secret that Google retains search data and meta-data regarding searches—in fact, it's quite open about doing so. What's unsure, though, is the long-term threat to information security and privacy.
Let's review Google's elements.

Google Search: This search engine is gathering many types of information about online activities. Its future products will include data gathering and targeting as a primary business goal.

All of Google's properties—including Google Search, Gmail, Orkut and Google Desktop—have deeply linked cookies that will expire in 2038. Each of these cookies has a globally unique identifier (GUID) and can store search queries every time you search the Web. Google does not delete any information from these cookies.

Therefore, if a list of search terms is given, Google can produce a list of people who searched for that term, which is identified either by IP address or Google cookie value. Conversely, if an IP address or Google cookie value is given, Google can also produce a list of the terms searched by the user of that IP address or cookie value.

Orkut: Google's social networking site contains confidential information such as name, email address, phone number, age, postal address, relationship status, number of children, religion and hobbies. In accordance with its terms of service, submitting, posting or displaying any information on or through the Orkut.com service automatically grants Orkut a worldwide, nonexclusive, sublicensable, transferable, royalty-free, perpetual, irrevocable right to copy, distribute, create derivative works of, and publicly perform and display such data.

Gmail: The primary risk in using Gmail lies in the fact that most users give their consent to make Gmail more than an email-delivery service and enable features such as searching, storage and shopping. This correlation of search and mail can lead to potential privacy risks. For example, email stored on third-party servers for more than 180 days is no longer protected by the Electronic Communications Privacy Act, which declares email a private means of communication.

Gmail Mobile: Mobile phones are increasingly being sold with Gmail built in, and if not, it can be downloaded. The questions to ask:

Please send your feedback, comments and ideas to me at raj@brainlink.com

95

How uniquely does your mobile phone identify you as the user, and when was the last time you changed your phone and your identifiers?

Gmail Patents: Gmail's Patent #20040059712 emphasizes "Serving advertisements using information associated with email." This allows Google to create profiles based on a variety of information derived from emails related to senders, recipients, address books, subject-line texts, path name of attachments and so on.

Google Desktop: Google Desktop allows users to search their desktops using a Google-like interface. All word-based documents, spreadsheets, emails and images on a computer are instantly searchable. Index information is stored on the local computer. Google Desktop 3 allows users to search across multiple computers. GD3 stores index and copies of files on Google's servers for nearly a month.

Chrome: Chrome is Google's browser. It's available for download today and will eventually be installed on new PCs. some of the risks it poses include:

- Every URL visited gets logged by Google

- Every word, partial word or phrase typed into the location bar, even if you don't click the enter/return button gets logged by Google

- Chrome sends an automatic

cookie with every automatic search it performs in the location bar

Android: Android is Google's operating system for cell phones. It retains information about dialed phone numbers, received phone-call numbers, Web searches, emails and geographic locations at which the phone was used.

Google Health: This product allows consumers—such as employees, coworkers and customers—to store their health records with Google. recently, CVs Caremark, along with Walgreens and Longs Drugs in the united states, agreed to allow Google Health users to import their pharmacy records.

Organizational Threats

uninstalling these products or using competitive tools can mitigate many of these threats. but what about the dangers to your organization? One example is Google search with its Google Flu Trends (www.google.org/flutrends).

Google has correlated flu data from the u.s. Centers for Disease Control (CDC) from 2003 to the present with its own search data. spikes in users' searches about flu treatments correlated tightly with the CDC data. Flu Trends has demonstrated Google's ability to analyze search data for a specific term or set of terms. And it can retain this data and where it came from because Google in its privacy policies states that it records IP addresses. so, what's to stop Google from analyzing all search data from your organization's networks? What's the difference between analyzing flu trends and "Top 100 search terms from xYZ Corp."? Or what if a company were to correlate regional threats from swine flu with search data from Google Health/Prescription data and then analyze the health of its employees and detect longterm effects?

Overall, the most critical threat is reliance on Gmail—whether the setting is universities, cities, companies or countries switching to Gmail en masse, or the newest employees in the organization using Gmail as their primary or sole email platform.

Questions to ask your security team: How big is the organization's email archive? How many years of emails are saved? If your organization switches its email hosting service to Google Gmail, what happens to the privacy and confidentiality clauses in your employee and customer contracts?

Another area of concern for hosted email is the potential of having to turn that data over to the government. Google, Yahoo and microsoft have a history of complying with the united states' and foreign governments' requests for information. If such data is turned over, how much corporate security is being eroded?

Consider the amount of money and manpower dedicated to handling microsoft Windows patches, viruses, spyware and botnet detection. Imagine the impact that reliance on Google products could have on corporate privacy and security.

Raj Goel, CISSP, is chief technology officer of Brainlink International, an IT services firm. He is located in New York and can be reached at raj@goel.com.

Please send your feedback, comments and ideas to me at raj@brainlink.com

Beyond Security Awareness

TALKING ABOUT SECURITY IS NOT ENOUGH. WE ALL NEED TO
ACT ON SECURITY PRACTICES.

RAJ GOEL, CISSP,
is CTO of Brainlink
International, Inc.
and an IT and
infosecurity expert
who develops security
solutions for various
industries. Senior
Managing Editor
Joyce Chutchian

spoke with Raj about the state of IT
security.

Q: *You've written and spoken a lot*
about social media threats and risks.
What are your biggest concerns?

First of all, there is the myth that
cybercrime and financial fraud
is a recent concept, when in fact,
the problems started in the 1934
to 1936 era, when the IRS issued
Social Security cards. Your Social
Security number became your de
facto ID number, and it's still used
today, despite all the corruption and
identity fraud.

I give a popular talk at conferences,
on how social media and the cloud
are over-collecting worldwide,
especially for the under-18

population. Kids who
were born in 1983 and
beyond have grown up
with computers. They do
everything online like
SMSing and chatting.
As teenagers, they are
not wired to think of
34-year-old threats. We
have built a surveillance
engine; everything a 12-year-old
says online will never be forgotten.
And what they say and what their
friends do and say, whether it be on
a game website, retail or Facebook,
will follow them and haunt them for
the rest of their lives. It's all stored in
the cloud, and they don't even know
what the cloud really is.

Q: *What are your biggest*
concerns about the cloud right now?

From a technical perspective, there
is no clear definition of what the
cloud is. Some people are relabeling
it as private hosting, and private data
centers are relabeling it as the cloud.
From a legal perspective— under
current U.S. federal law—what
the cloud gives you technically, it
takes from you legally. Take HIPAA

for example: You are a doctor. If your records go missing, you are personally liable for that data loss. The customer records are lost, and the organization is held accountable for any breached data.

In the cloud, if your vendor loses data, the vendor is not liable. You are liable. I'm working with nonprofit, underprivileged healthcare organizations, and they want to be compliant. They don't have the budget, so they are moving to Google Apps. Google says not to use Google Apps for HIPAA or PCI. Vendors have been carefully insulating themselves from any liability without telling the customer. There is no lemon law for cloud computing. If Google loses your data…oops! The liability is yours.

Q: What can we do about this?

We need to educate everyone aged 18 to 60. This means educate ourselves, management, families, and other members of our society who help enforce the laws, design and pass them. Don't just collect a paycheck. Be involved as citizens of our society and in politics. As security professionals, we are all citizens, and we are all consumers. It is our charter that we have to be in the front lines of protecting fellow citizens, whether it be attorneys, accountants, teachers, parents, medical professionals, etc. Go talk to your local parent/teacher school groups. Talk to the Boy Scouts and Girl Scouts; local attorneys and bar associations.

I have spent more than fifteen years reading the law on security—and it's not how you can configure a firewall, it's how you can create a security policy. Encrypt your laptop. Don't be lazy. It's not enough to be educated— you need to enforce awareness. Just because a security question asks you for your mother's maiden name, doesn't mean you have to use her real name. Change your passwords frequently. Don't just talk about security, act on it.

Issue Number 19 Infosecurity Professional

Please send your feedback, comments and ideas to me at raj@brainlink.com

☑ Penetration Testing
☑ Corporate Espionage
☑ Psychopaths

WELCOME TO THE WORLD OF
DATING SITES

XOXO, **RAJ GOEL**

SEVERAL YEARS AGO, New York photographer Nev Shulman fell in love with a woman named Megan, whom he met on Facebook. Over time, he began to wonder if Megan was perhaps being less than truthful, and, with a film crew, went to Michigan to track her down.

Instead of meeting the love of his life, Shulman came to realize he'd been having a relationship with a married woman named Angela, who had created Megan's profile (and more than a dozen others) to lure him into an online relationship.

Shulman documented the tale in a U.S. movie called *Catfish* and parlayed the film's popularity into a cable television series of the same name. In each episode, someone begins to suspect they are being duped by an online boyfriend or girlfriend they have never met in person. In most cases, their suspicions are confirmed by the end of the show.

Most of us shake our heads at people's gullibility, but the truth is, it is all too easy to fall victim, especially if we are actively looking for a meaningful relationship through the Internet. Whether it's match. com, eHarmony.com, okcupid.com, christianmingle.com, jdate.com for Jewish singles or shaadi.com for Indian families (or the hundreds of Chinese, Russian, and other regional and language-specific sites), there is an online community willing to play matchmaker.

But lonely hearts aren't the only ones on those sites. Predators, psychopaths, criminals, and even employers are lurking there, too, potentially taking advantage of what these sites and apps promise to deliver: potential companionship. But along with this promise comes a host of privacy and security threats. Most of us in IT security are well aware of the risks when dating online. Are your coworkers?

Private Isn't So Private

The real problem with most dating sites is the amount of information people post about themselves in order to find a suitable match. The questionnaires are legendary for their length and depth. And the responses create a profile that never goes away.

Some people, after creating a profile, end up in a relationship, but, more commonly, they abandon the site after a while and maybe delete the app. But do they remember to completely delete their profile? Those who don't likely do so partly from ignorance and partly from convenience in case they want to get back in the game and want to avoid the onerous process of filling in all those fields again. So, their profile is still alive and well and available to anyone who knows how to access it.

People who use the "let's-meet-up" app Tinder or Snapchat, a photo delivery app which promises that pictures will disappear on command from the recipient's cell phone, aren't any safer.

- In January 2014, 4.6 million Snapchat users had their data dumped on the Internet. As reported in the January 3, 2014 edition of Forbes.com, the data included usernames and partial phone numbers.

- In October 2014, a third-party app called Snapsaved was breached, and the often sexual photos of many Snapchat users were leaked. Pcmag.com reported on October 13, 2014 that nearly 200,000 photos had been leaked.

- A breach on the mobile dating app Tinder lasted approximately two weeks and leaked full name, date of birth and location, despite the app CEO's assertion that the breach was of a much shorter duration, as reported

Please send your feedback, comments and ideas to me at raj@brainlink.com

in the July 25, 2013 edition of qz.com.

So, how does all this pose security threats to the enterprise?

Online Dating – Toxic to the Workplace

Consider a corporate executive with a secret life. Professionally, she is easily tracked through her LinkedInprofile (which may be managed by her marketing department) and her bio on the company's website.

But what about her private online life, which includes profiles and photos on several dating sites? It's not difficult at all for anyone to put the public and private online personas together.

Most of the dating sites/apps expose her current physical location, marital status, sexual or dating preferences, things she likes to do for fun, and the type of person she likes to do it with. And this executive is likely to be a little more candid if she believes all of this information is safe from public view. And, she believes that lying to protect her identity defeats the purpose of finding someone with the same interests.

But the confluence of the two could impact her career, now and in the future. Employers also have been known to reject job candidates based on finding and reading the candidates' profiles on dating sites. A 2012 market study by Eurocom

Worldwide and reported in the April 2013 edition of Forbes.com revealed that one in five technology executives said that they had not hired a candidate because of what they saw in the candidate's social media profiles.

The Tricks of the Cyber Villains

This is not to suggest everyone who uses social media or dating sites is going to fall prey to scams or interlopers. We know from all of the success stories touted on television and radio, and perhaps among your networks of friends, that isn't the case. Dating sites have become an acceptable means of matchmaking in today's society.

However, it's important for everyone in your organization (and, quite honestly, extended families and friends) to be aware of the threats honey traps (use of attractive male or female spies to trap the victim to gain access they otherwise might never obtain) pose to them and their organization.

Penetration testers and criminals routinely create LinkedIn profiles of attractive female recruiters to conduct reconnaissance on their targets, as documented on techday. com. Sometimes they fabricate the information in a profile; other times it's lifted from other members' profiles. Some companies even post fake profiles to lure people into paying monthly fees for non-existent dates. In November, 2014, the U.S.

Federal Trade Commission (FTC) fined JDI Dating, a U.K.-based online dating site, for fabricating profiles and charging a fee to connect. On November 1, 2014 c/net.com reported that JDI was ordered to pay $616,165 for posting fake profiles.

Divorce, Cyber Style

Social media can also wreak havoc with your personal life. Match.com likes to tell you in their commercials that one in five marriages and relationships begin online. What they don't tell you is that in the U.S., according to a 2010 study by the American Association of Matrimonial Lawyers and reported in The Guardian on March 8, 2011, four out of five divorces begin with information found online. And in the UK, according to Divorce-Online, one out of every three divorces cites Facebook as the cause for divorce.

More and more matrimonial attorneys are now requiring that their clients given them their Facebook, Twitter, Gmail account credentials as part of the divorce process. In the July 19, 2013 edition of Family Lawyer Magazine, the authors advise their readers on how to mine their clients' (and their opponents') social media data to protect their clients (and find damaging data on the opposition).

How to Avoid Online Heartbreak—and Worse

That's the rub. And that's why so many people provide so much sensitive, private, valuable data— data that's also easily available to a penetration tester, social engineer, criminal, stalker, or opposing counsel.

Valentine's Day is approaching, and many of your colleagues (perhaps even you) will decide it's time to join a dating site. I strongly recommend that you educate yourself and your users about the long-term dangers of these sites.

A few tips:

- Ask them to keep track of which sites and apps they use. In a few weeks, remind them to delete accounts/profiles of sites they're no longer using.

- Keep an eye on your web traffic for new, interesting or suspicious dating websites and apps.

- Remind your users to avoid installing unapproved/ unauthorized apps on their corporate phones and tablets.

- With approval from management and legal, use data from social media and dating sites as case studies in your security awareness training.

- For parents of teens and tweens, have a conversation with them about emotional, reputational and legal dangers of social

Please send your feedback, comments and ideas to me at raj@brainlink.com

media, including sexting and Snapchatting.

Consider this a friendly reminder that the Internet has democratized crime, lowered the costs for conducting espionage and data theft, and made our jobs working in information security much, much more challenging.

As security luminary Dan Geer once said, "In the world of network computers, every sociopath is your neighbor."

RAJ GOEL, CISSP, is a New York-based cyber civil rights advocate, author, and speaker. He is the owner of Brainlink International.

IS SOCIAL MEDIA **TOO SOCIAL?** BY KEN NOVITSKY

IT HAPPENS. And it happens more often than you think. A comment on a friend's Facebook or hyperlink in a blog post lures you to click, and once you do, you instantly regret it.

This isn't remorse for what's written—or left unsaid—but for being duped into downloading malware, like "malvertising" that appears to buy traffic from legitimate ad providers in order to place malicious ads on popular YouTube videos. Before you know it, your machine's become part of a massive botnet. And it only gets worse, once your personal information is harvested and your online identity is used to find new victims.

There is nothing new about social engineering being used for clandestine information reconnaissance for an illegitimate purpose. But despite decades of warnings, malware still proliferates. And for several years now, social media has been the conduit of choice.

Giving Away Too Much

While most of us are now wary of emails from foreign princes needing to park some royal money, we aren't as suspicious when a request with a hyperlink comes from someone we know (or would like to know).

Yes, social media is a good place for the bad guys to leverage social engineering techniques to continue their attack. The more you expose yourself and your personally identifiable information to the world, the more susceptible you are to being used as a lure.

Typical information people share about themselves through social networks includes:

- Name and photo
- General location where they live, hang out and travel
- Employer and job title
- Professional skills and connections
- Prior employers
- Education, including schools and graduation years
- Personal interests/hobbies

And in some cases, we involuntarily share information such as user's IP address; host name; and URL history.

Know the Scams

All this information is a boon to those seeking to exploit it for nefarious purposes. It can be used to select targets and/or to create custom-tailored enticements or just plain, good old fashioned exploitation. A 2014 Symantec Intelligence Report listed the top five attacks or exploitations that can use this information:

Please send your feedback, comments and ideas to me at raj@brainlink.com

Fake Offers. These scams invite social network users to join a fake event or group, offering incentives such as free gift cards. Joining often requires the user to share credentials with the attacker or send a text to a premium rate number. This is the most common kind of attack, accounting for 52 percent of exploits.

Manual Sharing Scams.
These use the victims to do all the hard work of sharing the scam by presenting them with intriguing videos, fake offers or messages that they share with their friends. This is second most common type of exploitation (37 percent).

Likejacking. Using fake "Like" buttons, attackers trick users into installing malware and may post updates on a user's newsfeed, spreading the attack. This type of exploitation occurred 8.5 percent of the time.

Fake Apps. These are applications provided by attackers that appear to be legitimate but carry a malicious payload. The attackers often take legitimate apps, bundle malware with them, and then re-release them as a free version of the app. This accounts for 1.7 percent of exploitations.

Comment Jacking. Similar to likejacking, this type of scam relies on users clicking links that are added to comments by attackers. The links may lead to malware or survey scams. As an exploit, it's still uncommon, accounting for less than 1 percent of attacks.

Setting up a fake account and building trust with owners of valid accounts is also a way to spread malware. What better way to gain confidence than to pretend to be someone with whom your target audience would love to connect. And the more people connected with the legitimate the account, the better the odds of exploitation.

Another type of scam involves exploiting such trust but does not necessarily involve malware scenarios per se. For example, a common investment scam using social media, called a "Pump-and-Dump", is used to manipulate markets. "Pump-and-Dump" schemes involve trumpeting a company's stock (typically small companies) through false and misleading statements to the marketplace. These false claims could be made on social media, as well as on bulletin boards and chat rooms. Once these fraudsters "dump" their shares and stop hyping the stock, the price typically falls, and investors lose their money.

Take Control

So what can be done, especially given most of us want to build an online presence to improve our careers, maybe even our offline social lives?

First and foremost, keep up with software patches, especially those fixing vulnerabilities in web browsers.

Additionally, here are some suggestions from Microsoft's Safety and Security Center:

> **Be linkophobic!** Fear of links is good. Clicking on links can lead to bad things. This is probably the most common way that malware gets spread. No matter who sent it to you or where it is, use caution when clicking on it.

> **Be careful about what you post about yourself.** This may give someone potential insight into how to social engineer any security question you may have set up to prevent unauthorized access to your account. Along this line, it may be wise to setup "false" answers that only you would know to such security questions to thwart this kind of hacking.

> **Don't trust and try to verify.** This is a little different spin on the old proverb about trusting no one, even your mother, but it's just as valid when it comes to receiving email messages.

Thatemail you just received from your mom may very well be a malicious actor who has just hacked her account. Try calling her first to see if she really sent it, especially if it contains links.

Watch out for fake login pages. Clicking on links (in a phishing or bogus email) that appear to take you to a legitimate site login may very well bring you to a fake page that can capture your credentials. For example, a link showing "www.yourbank.com" may really take you to "www.captureyourpassword.com."

> **Don't accept just anybody's connection.** If you don't know the person or even if you do, make sure the account they are using is a real one. The days of trying to appear popular by "friending" as many people and connections as you can are over. It turns out that, just like real life, it's all about quality over quantity.

> **Read privacy policies, especially when there's a change.** Do not assume your content remains private if there are changes that reset accounts to more public modes. Is it fair? No, but it's your job to stay on top of privacy policy changes.

> **Remember—anything you post can be permanent.** There is no telling where that information

Please send your feedback, comments and ideas to me at raj@brainlink.com

will turn up in the future even though you thought you deleted it and it was long gone.

Practice safe hex! Be careful about installing that add-on when you can't be sure who wrote it and if it will do what it says it will do.

Avoid using social network sites at work. You might be opening a door allowing your network to be infected. You also may be violating your employer's Acceptable Internet Use Policy.

Perhaps this year, one of your personal goals is to become more social, or maybe it's to become less social and to focus on other pursuits besides updating your Facebook or Twitter accounts hourly or daily. Regardless of where you see yourself online in 2015, be smart about what and how you share and connect.

KEN NOVITSKY, CISSP, is an IT consultant for a major northeast utility. His work focuses on IT security issues as well as IT internal controls.

CHILD PORNOGRAPHY Q&A:
How To Protect
YOUR HOME AND BUSINESS

> *More people are killed every year by pigs than by sharks, which shows you how good we are at evaluating risk.*
>
> BRUCE SCHNEIER

Child porn is as prevalent as it is insidious, yet the majority of the public remains uneducated on how to handle the unexpected appearance of child porn on their devices. Raj Goel, one of the world's most respected cyber security experts, answers questions and offers guidance on this potentially very damaging issue.

Q: *Starting with an example from the real world, who is Leo Flynn, and what can we learn from his federal investigation?*

Raj: Leo Thomas Flynn is a criminal defense attorney working out of South Dakota who was tried for charges of child pornography. And in this particular case, under a state law as an attorney, he could do research on child porn in preparation for his case. Under his state law, that's allowed. And in some states, attorneys can look at child porn legally without getting in trouble with the state law or the state courts. Under federal law, however, any human being in the United States who had more than three pieces of what is determined to be child porn is guilty of possession of child pornography, which is a felony. And under federal law, if you get three or more pieces of child porn, you are supposed to stop everything, notify your local district attorney's office, and allow them to come and seize the technology.

Please send your feedback, comments and ideas to me at raj@braintlink.com

If an attorney is doing cyber forensics for a client, and they encounter child pornography, what is the attorney supposed to do? The correct legal answer is to stop everything and call the police. It's the federal law to do so, and failing to can result in arrest.

But many attorneys are under the impression that this would be covered under attorney client privilege. In most cases, if a client tells an attorney that they killed someone, what they have said to their attorney is legally protected speech. So attorneys are under a false belief that if a client gives them a hard drive full of child porn, or they do forensics analysis, that the crime occurred in the past. However, if you tell your attorney, "I'm going to kill somebody tomorrow," then the attorney is under legal obligation to notify law enforcement about a future crime or a pending crime. And under federal law, if you download child porn and you have it in your possession on your hard drive, in a forensics image, or in an email, that is a current and active case of possession and distribution.

In Leo Flynn's case, under his state law, he was allowed to do what he was doing. Under federal law, he wasn't. And for three years, the secret service and the US government dragged him through hell and high water, and he won his case on a very narrow technicality. Had he lost, a very well-respected attorney and expert on criminal defense would have been in jail for following state law, which is in conflict with federal law.

Q: *For average citizens whose work would not deal with child pornography, what are some ways that this still might be a concern for them?*

Raj: This is one area where we see a lot of businesses and families get into trouble. For example, if a girl in high school sends a nude photo to her boyfriend and he shares it with their classmates. Yes, it's harmful, degrading, and embarrassing to the girl. It's also a federal felony because every child who got that SMS message or email with the girl's photos is now guilty of possession of child porn. So you'll see many cases around the country where if the schools even suspect one child of passing around this type of material, they will notify all the parents and contact law enforcement. If your kid comes home with these images, and you look at it and it's got more than one photo, technically you're guilty of child porn possession. And the kids that don't report it can be charged with child porn possession and be labeled a sexual predator. So can kids who report it.

So my advice to most parents and business owners is: if you suspect child porn, find a good criminal defense attorney who knows how to deal with this kind of evidence. Then have them contact law enforcement. Calling the cops by yourself could get you in more trouble than it's worth. And you can't delete the files or not report it. If you delete those files on your kids' smart phones or their laptops, and it comes out later that you deleted the files, now you're guilty of not only possession of child porn but also deletion of evidence, which is another crime at a federal level.

Q: *And the risks and concerns are just as prevalent in a business environment, aren't they?*

Raj: Let's say that in a corporate environment you fire an employee for something standard such as being rude to a customer, and you discover child porn while going through his hard drive – if you then email those files to your attorney for review, you're now guilty under federal law of distribution of child pornography. And this is where a lot of corporate attorneys and business owners get into trouble. Another common mistake a lot of business owners make is if they find something, they'll have their IT guy to find stuff, or delete stuff. That actually makes the problem a lot worse. You as a business owner – and it doesn't matter what business you're in: you could be a florist, a banker, a realtor, an attorney – you should know what the federal and state laws are about cyber evidence, about what can and can't be done with a hard drive and who to call when you need to call them.

Please send your feedback, comments and ideas to me at raj@brainlink.com

Sending the photos to an attorney may appear to be the right thing to do, but doing that actually endangers you and your attorney. This is one of those areas of federal law which most people don't know about. Even most attorneys don't know about it, and this is where what you don't know can hurt you really, really badly.

Q: *If your child comes home with an inappropriate picture on their phone, what are the steps that a parent needs to take to handle the situation in the most efficient way?*

Raj: First thing first is: if they come home and you discover something on their phone – don't email it to your attorney or anybody else. If you think it's child porn, pull the plug right away. If it's a phone, take out the battery. If it's a laptop or desktop, take it off the internet, shut it down. Do not email these pictures to anybody else.

Secondly, contact a good attorney that you know and that you trust. Be sure to ask them if they are a criminal defense attorney and whether they have worked with child porn and sexual predator issues. If they're a good attorney they'll say if they have, or if they haven't they'll be able to recommend someone who has. Basically, hiring an attorney is like hiring any other professional. Interview the hell out of them. Just because they have an esquire after their name does not mean they're qualified to represent you in this particular matter, and you may have to go through a couple of people until you find somebody that is appropriate for you. They speak at your level, they understand where you're coming from, they fit your budget, they fit your needs, and they fit your worldview. The attorneys I like may not be the ones you like. It's like hiring any other professional, whether it's a doctor, realtor, or an IT guy. Talk to the people in your community and get some good references. And when you get a good attorney or you find somebody, have them submit recommendations to you. Ask them about their experience. Put them on trial before they put you on trial.

112

Q: For those that feel that hiring an attorney and a forensic specialist is too expensive, are there other options for resolving problems like these?

Raj: Great question. I get this a lot and honestly, I don't have a good answer. I'm not saying everybody should keep me on speed dial. There aren't too many of us in the country who are good at forensic analysis in the first place. There are very few people who do what I do and work in the private sector. But this is a case of damned if you do and damned if you don't. If you try to bury the evidence and try to ignore it, you risk doing a lot of damage to your reputation and public image once the case goes to trial and is picked up by the media. And whether you win or lose, every trial is an exhausting, expensive experience. And I hope people never have to hire me for forensics work because it's dirty, nasty, expensive, and usually not a pleasant experience for anybody involved. But if you don't educate yourself now and find a good criminal defense attorney and forensic specialist, you risk finding yourself in a bad situation and getting somebody completely incompetent who makes your case even worse. The only thing worse than not having an attorney is having a bad attorney.

Q: Is it perhaps better to contact a person like you first, and then contact an attorney?

Raj: No, if somebody contacts me directly, my first course of action is, "Who's your attorney? If you don't have an attorney, I can't talk to you because anything I say is not protected." So if you tell me that you found something on your child's phone that you think is child porn, I can't keep it a secret if I'm under oath. I have to tell them what I heard or what was told to me. I am not an attorney. You don't get attorney-client privilege working with me directly. When I work for your attorney, then you benefit from at least some portion of the attorney-client umbrella. If you don't have the money, in a lot of major cities there are a lot of nonprofit legal societies that will work with you.

Please send your feedback, comments and ideas to me at raj@brainlink.com

113

Also, make friends with local district attorney's office and local police long before you need to. If they know you and know you're a good person, they're not going to treat you as a suspect or as badly as they would if you were a complete stranger. Be a good citizen and know your local law enforcement. Know your local district attorney's office and detectives and make friends with them.

Q: *Going back to a business scenario, would the process be different for a business owner who discovers an employee is in possession of child pornography?*

Raj: Right, the fence poles are exactly the same as a business owner. Yes, you have a regular in-house contract attorney. You're going to use them for day-to-day work, but just because they're a good contract attorney or tax attorney does not make them a good criminal defense attorney. Make friends with a bunch of attorneys. What if your employee is accused of selling stolen merchandise through your company website? What if your employee is accused of running a brothel or an escort service through your company resources? At some point in your life as a business owner, you're going to get sued by an employee, or a customer, or a competitor, or the federal government. It's just like getting mugged. If you're in New York City, at least once in your life you're going to get mugged. So long before that happens, know a couple of good criminal defense attorneys. Make friends with them and know what their skill sets are.

Having a good employee handbook up front with good employee/ employer contracts is great. Have in your employee handbook what all the rules and policies are. Advise your employees that everything in the company belongs to the company: the smart phones, the desktops, the laptops. Anything on there can be subjected to surveillance and acquisition. And make sure your criminal defense attorneys know some good forensics investigators, and they know law enforcement officials who are familiar with these issues and are willing to give you advice.

I do a lot of public speaking for free or at low cost to attorney groups, accounting groups, and small business associations precisely because of that. So go network like any other resource. A good criminal defense attorney and a good forensics investigator and a good cop and a good federal agent are people you hope you never need, but you should know them long before you need them.

Q: *Considering that evidence of this nature is likely to be found on personal devices, this brings to mind the 4th amendment with unreasonable search and seizure. How is cyber security dealing with that?*

Raj: Well, government has always had a problem with the fourth amendment and unreasonable search and seizure. New technology makes it much, much easier for governments and other parties to collect data on us, so under federal law, if your car is parked in your driveway, it's private property. If it's parked in the streets, it's public property, or rather it's on public property, therefore it's searchable by law enforcement. And the FBI put 3,000 GPS trackers on people, either without warrants or without court consent, because they thought they might be terrorists. The FBI lost a case last month, and they have to turn off 3,000 GPS trackers. But law enforcement will always try to get as much data as they can.

Where the fourth amendment comes into consideration is when technology allows the government more access to what you feel is your private information. You go to Facebook, you mark something private because Facebook tells you it's private, and you don't know it's not unless you listen to your other security professionals. And even then, kids believe Facebook when it says things are private.

If it's on Facebook or Gmail or Twitter, if it's on the Internet, it's never going to get deleted, it's never going to be private, and even a harmless joke in the wrong context will be seen in the worst light possible. There's a man in Florida, a retired military person,

Please send your feedback, comments and ideas to me at raj@brainlink.com

who sent a Twitter post regarding Occupy Wall Street. I don't support his statement that 'nothing will change if we kill a cop'. I don't believe we should kill cops. He said it. I don't agree with the statement, but like Patrick Henry, I will defend his right to say it. It's free speech. If he takes a gun and kills somebody, that's murder, send him to jail. But he can say it. That's our first amendment right. But because he used Twitter to say it versus an open microphone, NYPD and law enforcement are now subpoenaing Twitter to find out who said this in Florida. Where do you draw the line between hateful speech and intimidation? It's a very interesting question for which I don't think anybody has a good answer.

Q: *Any final thoughts?*

Raj: In summary, there's nothing wrong with the tools. Facebook isn't a bad technology, and neither is Gmail or Twitter. So either we have to kill the technology or, better yet, upgrade the laws to take into account that what's in a smart phone, etc., should count as private property. And ask yourself, what can you, as an American citizen, do to safeguard the rights you have and to protect them for your children and your grandchildren?

NET NEUTRALITY
Q & A

> *The PATRIOT Act provisions relevant to [the NSA's surveillance]*
> *program expire on June 1st and the Senate needs to vote to extend*
> *the PATRIOT Act... Why should we allow the United States*
> *goverment to continue to infringe upon liberty?*
>
> THE DAILY SHOW WITH JON STEWART

Though it's certainly been a hot topic in recent years, net neutrality is not often fully understood. Noted cyber security and privacy law expert Raj Goel participates in a Q&A and shares his valuable insights on this topic below.

Q: In the Western world, we've grown accustomed to an open Internet, and we might have some difficulty understanding the necessity of protecting net neutrality. What would a world without net neutrality look like?

Raj: This might be surprising, but a great indication of what our lives would look like without net neutrality comes from the 19th century. In the 1860s, prior to the Civil War, the US had four or five different gauge sizes. The North had two different gauges: one for the railroads and one for the subway systems and so on. The South and the West had three different gauge sizes, and one of the reasons the South lost the war is because their trains and their supply lines could not transfer product fast enough. When the North won the war, one of the first things US Congress did was rebuild the Southern railroads to the Northern track size, which is why you can build products for anything in the country – except for mining tunnels and subway systems – from anywhere in the country.

Please send your feedback, comments and ideas to me at raj@brainlink.com

And that ties in with net neutrality. Net neutrality today, or the Internet, is no different than the railroads. It grew just as fast – faster, even – than the railroads did; it connected the world. The railroads connected the US, turning weeks and months of journey into a matter of days. The Internet collapses time and space so you can send an email to China in the same two seconds it takes to email the colleague in the cubical next door. What's happening now is we're going back in time, and corporations want to Balkanize the Internet because the more we are their captive audience, the higher they can raise our rates. The Apple iTunes store is a great example of this. What's the only currency allowed? iTunes credits. Who is the only governor on the Apple ecosystem? It's Apple. They don't like an app? They can revoke it. They don't like you? They can reject your applications. They can kick you off the network and kill you in the process. Same with Amazon and Kindle. Amazon doesn't like your book? They can pull it off, even if people already paid for it.

Q: And what do you mean by "Balkanize"?

Raj: Well, it comes from the Balkans region of Europe, which historically has been contested and fought over by every empire from the Romans to the Greeks to the Mongols and the Huns to the Russians, the Americans, and everybody else. And as a result, Eastern Europe has a mish mash of cultures, languages, religion, and warring factions that goes back thousands of years. Each empire has introduced their own rules and as a result, it's a complete mess out there. Take the US where 50 states have a common language, a common currency, common road signs; we have a lot more things in common than not. Compare that to Eastern Europe, where two neighboring regions might have completely different languages and religions, and they've had wars every decade for the last thousand years.

So when I say Balkanized, I mean different companies or different entities – companies, governments, other entities – who will break the Internet apart, enforce their rules, their language, their currency to the exclusion of everybody else. And in the last 12 months, what has surprised me completely is how quickly Facebook, Apple, Verizon, and these private corporations have gone on a warpath to fragment the Internet for their own private benefit. AOL did this in the mid-90s. They built their own parallel Internet, if you will. And now we have the nice, open Internet and in the last 12 months, Apple has taken a really big stab at walling off the iPads and the iPhones from everybody else in the app stores. Amazon is now filtering the Internet for everyone who uses Kindle devices. You got a Kindle Fire. What you also got free with your purchase is an Internet traffic sniffer that controls what you can and can't see, and there's no guarantee whatsoever that you will actually see the Internet that you want to see off of your Kindle devices. Amazon controls what you can see and what you can't see.

Q: *Is there a case to be made for getting rid of net neutrality?*

Raj: Not for adults. We already have a separate Internet for the military, Milnet. We have a separate Internet for high-speed research, Internet2. I could see a case being made for creating digital playgrounds for students and kids, but that's not what net neutrality is about. I don't see a good reason in the Western economies for Internet without net neutrality. It would be like saying, "Hey, we've got this great highway system in the US and in Europe. Let's break it up. Let's put toll roads every 10 feet. Let's change the road size. Let's change the gas and the tires required in every state. Wouldn't that be fun?" The only people making money in the short run will be the toll collectors and the gas and power vendors. In the long run, we all lose. If you're going to get rid of net neutrality and create these different standards and different rights of access, then you might as well take the state highway system and break it up into what it was before Eisenhower was elected president. Let's go back to different roads, different states, different tolls, different tire sizes, and see how much fun that is.

We're going backwards. We built an open network, everybody

Please send your feedback, comments and ideas to me at raj@brainlink.com

could be on it, and for a number of reasons and a number of good arguments: preventing spam, preventing crime, lowering the nuisance factor, making it safer – under all these rubrics we're now taking the reverse path of taking this open system which has common standards, common gauges, common technologies and then breaking it up now for no good public reason. I can't find a single redeeming feature of a Balkanized Internet.

Q: *What kind of changes would we see if net neutrality was to go away? What's at stake if we do lose it?*

Raj: In the short run, we would see higher costs for every one of us. Whether we're consumers paying our cell phone bill, our cable bill, or our Internet bill, whether we're corporations, it's higher expenses for those of us who don't control the cartel or the monopoly on the access. And in the long run, it gives unsavory characters overarching control over communications. India has a law they passed that requires Facebook and Google to block certain words and phrases. China has their own rules. Do we all want the rest of the world to play by the rules of the road in China or India or Brazil or North Dakota?

Q: *What can consumers and businesses be doing to protect net neutrality?*

Raj: The first step is to be an informed citizen and be active in politics. Net neutrality isn't the most exciting topic and in reality, most of the major media in the Western world is owned by a handful of corporations who have no interest in net neutrality. So like every other important issue of every era – Civil Rights, women's rights, voting rights – we the informed citizens have to get concerned and buy back our politicians. Al Franken and

Charles Schumer have done a really good job of fighting for the average citizen, and where possible, we should be buying back our politicians with votes and dollars.

There is something else you can do. Writing letters and calling your elected officials always works. But remember that social media is also very powerful. When one mother got on Facebook and started the "Transfer Your Bank Accounts" movement, Bank of America blinked and cancelled their debit card fees. What we need to do is endorse businesses that are actually supporting net neutrality. And the ones who are not, we need name and shame the guys who are trying to break the spirit of the Internet. We need to hold our corporations and governments accountable for their actions.

*Please send your feedback, comments and ideas to me at **raj@brainlink.com***

SMART CARS:
Unsafe at Any Speed

> Hacking the location data on a car is merely an invasion of privacy,
> whereas hacking the control system of a car would be a threat to life.
>
> WORLD ECONOMIC FORUM'S
> GLOBAL RISK REPORT 2015

In July 2015, Chrysler recalled 1.4 million vehicles (one of the *largest recalls* in Chrysler's history) for a software bug.

As reported in Wired Magazine, researchers were able to control the heating & cooling system, blast the radio, activate the windshield wipers, shut the car down...*from a laptop 10 miles away.*

I was driving 70 mph on the edge of downtown St. Louis when the exploit began to take hold.

> *Though I hadn't touched the dashboard, the vents in the Jeep Cherokee started blasting cold air at the maximum setting, chilling the sweat on my back through the in-seat climate control system. Next the radio switched to the local hip hop station and began blaring Skee-lo at full volume. I spun the control knob left and hit the power button, to no avail. Then the windshield wipers turned on, and wiper fluid blurred the glass.*
>
> *As I tried to cope with all this, a picture of the two hackers performing these stunts appeared on the car's digital display: Charlie Miller and Chris Valasek, wearing their trademark track suits.*

Chrysler's solution to all this is to tell their customers to either bring the car to a local dealership (good idea!) for a software patch, or car owners can download and compile their own patches (dangerous idea!) or Chrysler will mail them USB keys (really, really dumb idea!).

I wonder how many Chrysler owners will ruin their cars by incorrectly applying the patch…or failing to apply it at all?

Chrysler isn't alone in software stupidity…

As reported in ZDNET, Samy Kamkar's OWNSTAR gadget allows anyone to locate, unlock, or remote start any GM vehicle by intercepting and breaching security of the RemoteLink mobile app.

Not one to rest on his laurels, Samy Kamkar further modified Ownstar to remotely hack into BMW, Mercedes-Benz and Chrysler vehicles.

As reported in Forbes, auto manufacturers aren't the only ones rolling out faulty code on America's roads. Progressive Insurance has placed up to 2 million vehicles at risk of shutdowns, thefts or mysterious accidents by sending drivers the **"Progressive Snapshot"** dongle. A gadget you plug into your car's OBD port. And while Snapshot promises "This little device turns your safe driving into savings", what it actually delivers is an insecure, easily hacked device that could lead to mayhem all across America.

Software has penetrated every facet of our society from computers to phones to TVs, microphones, houses, home security systems, cars, banks, power grids, etc. We cannot live without software.

The question is, how can we live with insecure, unsafe software?

How many people have to die, or get injured in preventable accidents before we take insurers, software developers and auto manufacturers to task?

Perhaps it's time to rename MADD as "Mothers Against Dangerous Developers".

Please send your feedback, comments and ideas to me at raj@brainlink.com

Action Items:

Read:

- *http://www.wired.com/2015/07/hackers-remotely-kill-jeep-highway/*

- *http://www.bbc.com/news/technology*

- *http://www.zdnet.com/article/ownstar-the-gm-onstar-connected-cars-worst-security-nightmare/*

- *http://arstechnica.com/security/2015/08/simple-wi-fi-attack-grabs-bmw-mercedes-and-chrysler-cars-virtual-keys/*

- *http://www.forbes.com/sites/thomasbrewster/2015/01/15/researcher-says-progressive-insurance-dongle-totally-insecure/*

FINAL
Thoughts

In every generation, a new King John, a new Khruschev, and a new Solzhenitsyn is born. It's OUR job as citizens to DEFEND the rights given to us by our respective constitutions and DEMAND that they be conferred on our WEAKEST citizens, not just the strongest or the wealthiest.

Privacy is a human right...
not a luxury for the selected few.

Please send your feedback, comments and ideas to me at raj@brainlink.com

THANK-YOU

I hope I have entertained you, educated you and caused you to take some action.

Any action you take to improve our civil society is a good one.

As I have said in many chapters, I would love to hear from you. Love the book? Get some idea out of it? Want some help in implementing them? Have some other stories I should know about? I want to know.

I travel all over the world speaking, writing and meeting awesome human beings. If I'm ever in your city, or you visit mine, connect with me and I'll buy you a cup of coffee.

My email is **raj@brainlink.com**
My twitter handle is **@RajGoel_NY**
My LinkedIn URL is **www.linkedin.com/in/rajgoel/**
My personal site is **www.RajGoel.com**

Take the chapters or stories you liked, photocopy them and share them at the family dinner table. Share the chapters (or the book) with your local school, discuss it at the next PTA meeting, and discuss it in Social Studies class.

You & I have benefitted greatly from the courage and sacrifice of thousands before us, who created the great American Experiment. Who created an amazing, enduring civil society. Let's do our part to preserve the constitutional and civil rights of our children, grandchildren, nieces, nephews, and neighbors.

Thank you for reading.

Made in the USA
Middletown, DE
16 October 2015